Rookie Police Experiment

Vol 1

Big City, Crime-Ridden Ghetto, 147 Rookies,
No Veterans, What Could Go Wrong

Michael Cubbage

Cover photograph: © Michael Cubbage, 1977

Library of Congress Control Number (LCCN): 2025916964.

Title: Rookie Police Experiment Vol 1

Subtitle: Big City, Crime-Ridden Ghetto, 147 Rookies, No Veterans, What Could Go Wrong

Publisher of Record:

Variation-A Publishing
An imprint of Variation-A, LLC
Palm Coast, Florida, USA
variationa.com

Paperback: 979-8-9933554-0-5

EBook: 979-8-9933554-1-2

Hardcover: 979-8-9933554-3-6

I dedicate this book to all those who, day after day, week after week, and year after year, don the uniform and equipment of law enforcement.

It's especially dedicated to those brave few who went directly from the police academy into a district void of veteran officers, accepted the baton and carried on.

They did this unrecognized, in a boldly conceived, never before attempted, yet to be repeated, and extraordinarily exciting experiment in law enforcement history.

Table of Contents

Acknowledgements

Kate Ward-Gaus, David Burns and Jude McKenna are the three busiest people I know, yet they still took the time to pre-read my first book and were kind enough to do the same for this two-volume piece. I gratefully appreciate their help and their many thoughts, suggestions and corrections.

They made the process more interesting, interactive and fun.

I must also acknowledge my wife Pat. She went through all of this with me, with never the slightest whimper of the fear she experienced every time I left for work. Notwithstanding forty-eight years and counting, putting up with me!

Introduction

This is an unusual book about an unusual person in an unusual situation.

If a *normal* person ✕ unusual situation = surreal, then this was surreal[très bizarre].

I've seen mock-ups of what Hollywood imagines it *might* be like for someone like me in a big city police department. This is what it was really like. To make it more interesting, the department ran a never-before-attempted, boldly conceived experiment in law enforcement just as I hit the street.

Beginning in 1971, The Pennsylvania Crime Commission began an investigation into corruption, resulting in what appeared as constant sweeps and arrests of police officers through one area of the city: the 17th Police District.

They categorized the corruption as *"... ongoing, widespread, systematic, and occurring at all levels..."*[1]

I felt like it was constantly in the news, and outside law enforcement agencies seemed to be running nets through it bi-annually.

In the early 1970s, I overheard a conversation when a recently retired police officer discussed the situation. He couldn't understand it either. As quickly as the authorities arrested police officers, there were applications to replace them.

He asked one police officer why he requested a transfer to a constantly raided district.

---

[1] PENNSYLVANIA CRIME COMMISSION - REPORT ON POLICE CORRUPTION AND THE QUALITY OF LAW ENFORCEMENT IN PHILADELPHIA
NCJ Number 25640 Author(s) ANON Date Published 1974 https://ojp.gov/ncjrs/virtual-library/abstracts/pennsylvania-crime-commission-report-police-corruption-and-quality#:~:text=THE%20COMMISSION%20FOUND%20THAT%20POLICE%20CORRUPTION%20IN,RANGING%20IN%20RANK%20FROM%20POLICEMAN%20TO%20INSPECTOR

He couldn't believe the answer he got, "I need the money."

In 1977, the 17th was again the focus of a corruption investigation, resulting in three more arrests. The commissioner transferred all veteran officers out of the district.

In a final effort to stem the corruption, the commissioner replaced them with newly minted police officers directly from the police academy.

That's what it seemed like then.

In retrospect, I can see they had been planning it for years. Quite cleverly, in fact.

They chose a newly minted captain to head the experiment. Rumor suggested the promise of a promotion if he could endure a year in this assignment.

That's the unusual situation.

Now for the unusual person:

Diagnosed with Asperger syndrome in 2014, shortly after my 60th birthday, I had endured six decades wondering what was wrong with everyone around me.

Nobody knew what Asperger syndrome was in 1977. Bumping around in the haze of social interaction with normal humans is difficult knowing what it is, but not knowing compounded the issue. Had anyone known *then*, you would not be reading this book *now*.

Pssst, fellow Aspies, *Don't tell anyone.*

I'm going to take you on a journey of anecdotes with the added twist: I should never have been there for more reasons than one. The already tenuous idea of sending brand new police officers into this situation would have been harrowing if everything was routine, but this place was über-corrupt. A normal veteran police officer would have their hands full.

I faced challenges among normal people in normal situations. This was a surreal adventure. I describe it in raw terms.

Coming from an environment requiring standardized test scores above the 95th percentile, leaving peers in Wharton and the Philadelphia College of Pharmacy & Science, I dove into the deep end of a situation, working with folks, some of whom were functionally illiterate, servicing folks who were 100% illiterate. I did this dragging with me what one of the foremost experts on the subject calls a devastating handicap.[2]

The 17th District was this experiment's laboratory. The experiment started, results recorded, and lessons learned, but unlike the labs most folks experience, many subjects in this lab were interactive, unpredictable, and often armed and dangerous.

The independent variables of the experiment were unpredictable, arbitrary and fast as a speeding bullet.

[2] Autism and Asperger syndrome - Edited by Uta Frith - MCR Cognitive Development Unit, London - Cambridge University Press, 1991, P. 5

Terms, My Definitions

Most are unfamiliar with Aspergers, so I created some definitions. These are my definitions and are what I mean as I tell my story. I'm fully aware they appear in other tomes with different meanings, but in the context of this book, this is what they mean:

Asperger syndrome-A social disorder caused by a brain variation limiting the ability to auto-process and apply social norms within the larger society. This is the standard I use in the book.

AS-Acronym for Asperger syndrome, appears differently elsewhere, but in this book, it means Asperger syndrome.

Asperger-This is what German-speaking people call a person identified with Asperger syndrome. Hence the title of the article, "Hans Asperger, selbst ein Asperger?" (Was Hans Asperger himself an Asperger?)

Aspie-This is what some of us call ourselves informally. It's our term. Only we may use it. It's like a *cop*. Only cops may use the word cop.

Note to the Reader

When I finally began to assemble *my story*, I found myself with such an abundance that I made decisions where one book ended and another began. My first book, "Aspergers. What's *Your* Excuse?" spans the time from the crib to the academy. Although I published that book first, I wrote this one first. After I finished this book, I proactively wrote the prequel.

I wrote in my first book:

Eidetic memory is good news, bad news. The good news is you remember pretty much everything, the bad news is you remember pretty much everything.

This is the first of two volumes recounting my years in uniform – beginning in the academy and ending with my promotion to detective. I changed the names of some characters for privacy reasons, but the stories are as I remember them. I played around with some timelines for the same reasons.

This is not a treatise on Asperger syndrome, but anecdotes of my life with enough info sprinkled in to show *where* one element affected the other. The treatise on Asperger syndrome is the focus of a future piece, where I explain the *why*.

I'm not on a spectrum, and I'm not autistic, so those terms won't appear in this text connected to Asperger syndrome. Other authors use the terms interchangeably. My belief is Asperger syndrome is a distinct human *variation:*

Variation-A.

Autism is something altogether different.

I dispensed with the many buzzwords such as neurodiverse and neurotypical because, frankly, there aren't as many as two consistent definitions of any of these terms. I limit references in this book to salient stereotypes and diagnostic criteria to point out the unique interaction of

AS with the anecdote without weighing the story down with technical detail.

In this book, anyone who is not an Asperger I refer to as a *normal* person.

As you read the stories, keep this in mind: It's not your normal person doing all this.

Prologue

Dinner in a high school cafeteria might not be your first choice for fine dining, but when it's on the set of *Rocky II* and includes lobster Newberg and the company of Hollywood Stars, it ain't bad. As the movie's scenes moved around Philly, the venues changed, but the food and company were consistently outstanding.

The extra attention I gave my uniform, often ostracized by my fellow police officers, paid off when my Lieutenant chose me as Silvester Stallone's bodyguard for the duration of the Philadelphia scenes for the movie.

After making sure that Sly, as I like to call him, had settled and, as much as he could, was enjoying his meal, I finally sat down to have mine. You see, Silvester Stallone wrote, directed and starred in the movie.

I no sooner got situated and reached for my napkin when a gentle voice caressed my ears with the question, "Is anyone sitting here?"

What happened next was mesmerizing. I looked up into the most beautiful face ever and momentarily froze before responding, "No, please have a seat."

The thoughts racing through my head ran from *"Where did they get such an angelic creature as this?"* to *"How on earth did they make her look so dowdy for the movie?"*

Talia Shire, Adrian to *Rocky* fans, has a face like a China Doll. It was like seeing the ballet for the first time, a visual feast. I stared, transfixed by her charming personality. My paradigm was big stars were cold and distant.

Then Burt Young appeared and asked if he could sit there too. He shattered the paradigm. This Pauly was nothing like the one you saw in the film. He was a soft-spoken, gentle, warm and lovable person.

After brief introductions, we sat, ate, conversed and enjoyed a nice dinner. Adrian and Pauly became my meal partners for the duration, never changing that gentle persona.

Now, how does this happen, you wonder. How does the Aspie get to do this job? And why did Adrian and Pauly remain my meal partners?

I think the idea of having someone *not* faun and fuss over you is sometimes refreshing to a big star. Treating them like normal folks gave them time to just sit, eat and relax.

If I jumped up like a normal person and asked for autographs and photos, I really believe they would have found a more peaceful place to have their meals.

This theme will show up frequently in the following stories. As an Aspie, I didn't recognize fads, trends or other *normal* behavior, nor did I think of celebrities as anything other than just people.

Chapter 1

Door to the Academy

On Wednesday, July 6, 1977, while Son of Sam terrorized NYC, and San Francisco searched in vain for the Zodiac Killer, I stood at the doors of the Philadelphia Police Academy for the first time as a cadet.

Dressed in the uniform, everyone called a waiter's costume, of a white dress shirt, plain black pants and shiny black shoes, my expectations were high. I would not be disappointed.

I strode past Spartan-clad classmates, casually chatting or tentative of entering. The expectation on my face clearly shone in the large mirror in the hall beyond the threshold where bold lettering urged a check of haircut, uniform, equipment, and pride.

I could feel the honest smile.

Past the mirror, I stepped into a large hall made of the same shiny beige porcelain bricks used to create most big-city police stations. Built for assemblies, a stage sat where the judge's pulpit would usually be in a roll call room. Roll call rooms were the multi-use rooms found in every police district station or headquarters.

Arranged in rows of familiar cold beige folding chairs were 100 places for us, reminiscent of those 100 seats in my first grade. But these seats were for adults who ranged in age from twenty to thirty-five, who chose to endure a two-year wait, leaving other jobs and situations to be here.

At 8:00 AM, the academy staff called 100 upturned faces to attention. We swore in as the newest police officers in Philadelphia. 94 shiny boyish faces and six brand new female police officers. These six were the second class of women to go through the academy as police officers.

They were *our girls.* (Get over it.) To them, we were *the boys.*

Then, as, what normal people would describe as reality settled in, hand-outs appeared.

Apparently, when we swore in, we magically became non-civilians. The handout explained as police officers, we could no longer gamble, drink in bars, cheat on our wives, politic, nor could we vote in uniform. There was to be no smoking in public while in uniform, no outside jobs without permission, and fifty other restrictions.

This was a major pivot point in my life, as I traded a society of haphazard chaos for one with clearly defined rules. And which, since I rarely drank, never smoked or gambled, and didn't have a wife, seemed perfectly in line with *my* thinking.

Amid the audible moans among the class, as they read the list, I became increasingly encouraged, and as reality set in for them, expectations rose for me.

A group of instructors took the stage. A police lieutenant tapped a microphone for quiet.

Flanked by instructors of various ranks, he said, "Ok, ladies and gentlemen, you'll be here for the next four months. During that time, there will be no days off without permission, and permission requires a memo to the commandant. No one is to carry a gun or get into any kind of trouble whatsoever, or you're gone."

This elicited more moans, quickly dissolved by glaring looks from the other instructors on the dais.

He continued, "This class is special in the history of the department. You are the first class of raw scores from the test, that is, the first class who did not receive the 10 extra military veteran-preference points. This class is predominately non-veteran."

"Every class before this one was 90% military veteran, but in this class, there are only six."

"Another special thing about this class is over 50% of the class have college degrees, also a first. Of the remaining, most have at least two years of college, and there are several with master's degrees, one PhD and one cadet in the third year of law school. We expect great things from this class."

Four months later, the lieutenant again spoke down from the dais, "This is the absolute *worst* class to attend the academy. You caused more mischief and trouble than any previous class."

Joe's familiar baritone sent back the reply, "That's what you get when you start hiring smart people."

In the retrospective I alluded to earlier, they were waiting for us.

Chapter 2

The Academy

Many characterize Aspergers as emotionless. I'm not emotionless, but I didn't expect to become any more nostalgic about the academy than I already was about grade school, high school or the three colleges I struggled through. I did, however, have expectations I would at least complete it because the light at the end of this tunnel was tangible and much closer.

A typical day began by swimming through the smokers at the front door into a building reminiscent of utility buildings you see along the highway where plows and salt trucks rust in summer.

The academy maintained lots of grass, an obstacle course, and one of the best pistol ranges in the country. Instructors made it a point to tell us that all the law enforcement personnel in the immediate area, including the local FBI, did their firearms training at our academy.

There were daily classes teaching us the Crimes Code[3], Motor Vehicle Code, Patrol Techniques, and Departmental Processes and Procedures.

The motor vehicle code instructor, with an indecipherable speech impediment, stood for an hour and read straight from the manual. I opened my manual in *subtitles mode* to understand him.

---

[3] Pennsylvania Crimes Code and Criminal Procedure 1976 - Official State Police Manual Copyright 1976 - Eleventh Edition. (The "Crimes Code" was the manual of PA laws that we were issued in the academy. It was our rules for enforcing the law.)

"An *implement of husbandry* must be yielded to when displaying the triangular caution marker." That was so memorable I just typed it by rote, a testament to the excitement of this subject.

Someone said, "A *what* of *what?*"

A cadet who was following along in the manual enunciated, "Implement of husbandry."

The first said, "What the heck is that?"

"Farm machinery, like a tractor."

"Oh, this is useful. When was the last time you saw a farm tractor in Philly?"

A self-styled comedian in the class constantly asked, "Could you please repeat that." Until he got the instructor to the point of a red-faced meltdown.

The other *academics* went similarly swimmingly. The Crimes Code lectures were equally dry. I found myself wondering about the significance of telling us the penalties for each of the crimes since it was on the other side of the process. I don't think I ever saw a person sentenced.

To sum up the academics, I attended classes, skimmed some of the books, did my best to stay awake and graduated 13 out of 100.

Overall, this experience was just a holding pattern for me. The real value was the friendships I was making in the four months I was there. Only fully realized after we left.

There were special sessions for driving, shooting, riot techniques, self-defense and first aid.

The instructors held driving class on top of a city reservoir. They decorated the raised flat surface with the area of a football field with snazzy orange traffic cones, designing a serpentine course.

We practiced negotiating the course with a police patrol car.

They demonstrated how the lights worked, the roof lights and the special large lights installed inside police cars that facilitated paperwork. We could disable this if we wanted to open the doors and not alert a bad guy.

They taught the use and function of the *siren head*, the small box inside the car, which controlled both the siren on the roof and the police radio. We tested the different sounds: the usual warble used by patrol cars and the long wail used by rescue units. This would come in handy later to fool the bad guys. Using the wail sounded like rescue coming rather than the police.

The siren-head contained dials to select different *bands* or frequencies. Each *division* claimed its own radio band. The city contained multiple *divisions,* each containing several *districts*. For example, West division, where I grew up, contained four districts: the 12th, 16th, 18th and 19th.

There were also special purpose bands: *J* for city-wide broadcasts and *H* for use by special units, such as *Night Command*, the uniform branch of Internal Affairs, so they could communicate with each other without the regular police officers hearing.

The staff taught when and how to use the police radio and the rules for using the lights and siren. We tested our *radio voices* via transmissions to the city-wide band. We learned that although we could hear the other cars communicating with the *dispatcher*, the official *voice* of police radio, we must not talk directly to them but through the dispatcher.

The dispatcher talked to the individual patrol cars, who responded to the dispatcher. Only supervisors may speak *car-to-car*. But even they usually spoke through the dispatcher.

Everyone performed well until the instructor turned on the lights and siren for the second round of the driving course. It was amazing and amusing to watch the effect.

Almost everyone knocked over the cones whenever they came to a curve or serpentine. I was surprised by the effect of the siren.

I went through it like it was a normal drive. This is one of the first indications of an applicable AS skill to the job. The fact I have no *fight-or-flight* response made it easier for me to respond to danger with unruffled feathers, a practical use of *the flat affect*.

Chapter 3

The Mile Run

Eidetic memory is good news, bad news. The good news is you remember pretty much everything, the bad news is you remember pretty much everything.

- The Author

Among those anomalies, *learn-ed people* call savant skills is eidetic memory. Many confuse this with photographic memory because memories are pictures or videos, the latter being a closer characterization, as they include input from all the senses, not *just* the visual.

When I recall an event or *playback the video*, I remember many more details because all senses are involved. This brings comments from others such as, "I remember the event, but not that level of detail." or more often, "How do you know all that?"

A lost art prevalent in that period was bathroom art. This was not graffiti or vandalism in the strictest sense but an accepted *artistic expression* found in almost every public restroom.

Bored in the assembly one morning, I doodled a poem I had read years before in the men's room on the second floor of Temple University's Speakman Hall:

A tiny bird with a yellow bill

Perched upon my windowsill

I lured it to me with bits of bread

And twisted off its little head.[4]

A cadet, Pete, who sat cattycorner to my right, nudged me for the paper. I handed it over. He laughed so loud that he startled the instructor, who stopped lecturing.

Pete and I became fast friends. We played off each other like a comedy team and spent much of our academy time together.

Physical training, or *PT,* consisted of: *the mile run, the obstacle course and hand-to-hand combat.* We received grey T-shirts, blue gym shorts, and a grey sweatsuit. The shirt and sweatsuit top read PHILA PD in PD Blue. The sweatsuit was the old heavy cotton type with elastic waist and ankles.

There were no showers like you see in the T.V. cop shows, so they held PT at the end of the day to limit the presence of sweaty cadets for the short time it took them to get to their cars and go home.

The max time for the mile run was six minutes. It was boring and consisted of trudging down the concrete sidewalk beside the Academy's plain galvanized cyclone fence.

Pete and I ran it together and qualified the first time around. Once you qualified, the cadre left you alone to concentrate on slow runners.

Two of the women approached us and said that one of the others was having a hard time passing the run. They nominated us to *do something,* so we connived a stunt. (This is something I never understood, but it happened a lot. My best guess is I was someone who would listen. An Aspie trait, most guys ignored them.)

---

[4] U.S. Army Marching cadence.

There was an official qualification at the end of the course, with sufficient notice, so you could achieve your best time. After Pete and I qualified, during subsequent runs, we ran to the end of the straight-away to the first turn on a street, hidden from the academy staff by a large fence.

We would stop and wait there.

The woman was overweight. They admitted her with the promise she lose the excess weight during the academy. She ran at a considerably slower pace; when she came around the corner, we would bracket her, grab her under the armpits and run her to the next turn.

The staff couldn't understand why it took her three minutes to run two legs of the run, but only one minute to run the leg behind the fence, which was the same distance. They suspected, but never bothered to check, so we kept doing it.

Unfortunately, she never lost sufficient weight. The academy dismissed her before we could perfect the stunt to the point where she qualified.

We tried.

Chapter 4

Obstacle Course

Two women couldn't vault the 6-foot-high wall in the obstacle course. This seemed like a useless exercise till I graduated. There are many areas of the city with alleyways behind their houses. There are small yards in the back separated by 6-foot-high fences.

I pursued several bad guys into alleys when we hit the street and watched them vault those fences. I realized I could run the outer edge and *watch them* vault the fence, catching them at the end of the row.

Like the run, you could qualify on the first try, and although required to run it each time, once you qualified, the cadre ignored you.

The front of the wall in the obstacle course was in direct line with the cadre with the clipboard. The back of the wall was like the far side of the moon to them, like the back fence in the mile run.

Pete and I would run the path to the back of the wall and wait. When the women came up, we would grab them one at a time and throw them to the top of the wall. They would grab the top, and we would push the bottoms of their feet up so they could get a leg over.

And, since almost anyone can fall off the top of a wall, they could navigate the rest themselves. Then, we would climb over ourselves.

They passed.

Honestly, I think the academy staff knew this was happening, too.

A similar issue arose at the fire academy. We spent a week at the fire department's academy learning how to react to fires. We learned about backdraft, when the force of the air feeding the fire could suck you into the blaze, as well as how to judge the intensity of a fire on the other side of a door by feeling the surface.

We learned about accelerants, such as gasoline and other flammables used in arson. We saw crime scene photos where arsonists used fires to hide evidence of homicides or insurance fraud.

Finally, we trained on ladders. The way this went, and I saw this on the street later, was the fire department would respond to a call from us. They would put the ladder up, smile and step back, saying, "There you go."

Then, we climbed to the roof to chase the bad guys.

Pete and I were at the top of the ladder inside the second floor of the mock house the firefighters used to train. We were all supposed to go up the ladder and into the second-story window and come back down.

Going up is easy; getting back down not so much.

Looking out that window and putting yourself back on the ladder to climb down was nerve-wracking. If you couldn't or wouldn't do this, however, they would kick you out of the academy as a coward.

All of us got in the window OK, but two women refused to get back on the ladder to go down. We told them to cover their eyes, and Pete and I picked them up and put them on the top of the ladder. We got away with this because the top of the ladder was inside the window, so we were partially hidden.

Once on the ladder we told them to stare straight ahead, move one hand to the next rung, one foot to the next rung and so on. In this way, they were able to pass this part of the training.

There were also guys who were afraid to get on the ladder, but we told them they were on their own. It was creepy enough for us to do it ourselves, let alone for these crybabies.

Chapter 5

Ginger Nightsticks

Unfamiliar equipment began to show up about three or four weeks into the academy. Unfamiliar to civilians recently turned police cadets, that is. I saw them unloading it in the shed, to me just another day, to the training cadre, another chance to nudge us.

The classrooms were rectangular boxes with linoleum tile floors and suspended ceilings. The chairs were the tan metal folding type you see in church cellar activity centers and the like.

During class that day, they issued equipment. This repeated itself for several days until we were proud owners of new batons, blackjacks handcuffs, and handcuff cases.

Baton was the official name for what we called a *nightstick* or simply *stick*. It was a twenty-two-inch-long hardwood stick. The *blackjack,* or *jack* as we called it, was a sixteen-ounce piece of cylindrical lead with a spring embedded in one end encased in leather. Electric stun devices and pepper spray replace both these days.

Most of the equipment was the usual uniform stuff. Nickle-plated handcuffs, leather handcuff cases and brown wood sticks. Equipment trickled in over the course of the first two months.

Two academy staffers sat at a table, and we queued up. They threw most of it at us, but since the handcuffs bore serial numbers, they collected our names for the record. This is in case a prisoner escapes with your handcuffs on; you are accountable.

Tom was in front of me in line. He was the only other red-head in the class. We were often confused one for the other.

13

The staffers saw him reach the table, then looked at each other and laughed. They handed him all his gear except a stick.

Tom asked, "What about a stick?"

They snickered and reached behind them to a separate box. From it, they produced two nightsticks made from a different kind of wood or stained differently than the others.

Everyone else got a *brown* stick. Tom and I were issued *red* ones.

They were not red like fire engines. They appeared to be from a different kind of wood with an auburn color like, well, our hair. They thought they were hilarious.

Tom said something smart to them. I took mine and left.

I can clearly see myself back in my seat tattooing my badge number into the wood of my new stick with the engraved ballpoint pen I got as a gift when I entered the academy, and clearly hear Louis remonstrating me for doing it.

Lou sat directly in front of me. He turned and said, "I don't think you should be doing that."

I said, "I'd rather get in trouble for this than for losing the stick."

I lost track of that stick after my promotion to detective because detectives don't carry sticks. That was 1980. In 2016, I got a call from Ed asking, "What was your cop badge number?"

He said, "I think Herc has your stick from the academy."

We met the next weekend, and sure enough, Herc presented the stick with the number where I tagged it in 1977, 39 years earlier.

I still have it.

Chapter 6

Please Uncuff me so
I can go to Lunch

Now in the classroom, everyone was clicking the handcuffs, poking their neighbor with the sticks and tapping exposed elbows with blackjacks.

I put the handcuff case on my belt and put the cuffs away. I put the case upside down. My thought was it would be easier to get the cuffs out this way.

At lunchtime, everyone bolted out of their seats for the door.

I noticed Lou didn't get up and said, "Let's go, Lou."

He gave me a funny look.

I said, "What's wrong?"

He motioned with his head I should look behind him. Someone handcuffed him to the chair.

I said, "What the heck?"

He said, "Someone asked to see my cuffs, and he and Bobby cuffed me to the chair."

I shook my head. I uncuffed him, and we went to lunch.

Chapter 7

Lawn Darts

After lunch, Pete and I contributed to the pranks that would later prompt the lieutenant's remarks about us being the worst class. According to some experts, Aspies' social development stalls at age 17. This was *definitely* a teenage stunt.

We were outside on the large lawn beside the academy building in some holding pattern between classes, and I noticed the ground was soft from a recent rain.

I motioned to Pete. I said loudly enough for the nearby cadets to hear. Holding the blackjack up as if I was admiring it, "You know what this is?"

"No, what is it?"

"It's a lawn dart."

"How so?" asked Pete

"Watch," I responded.

I took the blackjack, which is top-heavy, and threw it overhand to the middle of the lawn, halfway between where we were and the side of the building. It flew in an arch, righted itself due to the balance issue, and stuck in the lawn.

Pete nodded and did the same.

Then, we retrieved the jacks and pantomimed what we did on the way back. We held a discussion about their flight characteristics and techniques of throwing. All the while watching the actions of the other cadets from our periphery.

Several of the other cadets, seeing this, were lightly slapping the jacks against their hands, testing their flightworthiness. Others were dropping them to judge how they would land.

Then, one of the cadets launched his.

Pete and I quickly stepped to the back of the crowd.

Within seconds, there were dozens of jacks flying. The atmosphere got loud and party-like as more wanted to try their skill at this newly discovered form of lawn darts.

The noise attracted the academy staff who went as ballistic as the jacks. Pete and I watched from a safe distance.

Chapter 8

Pistol Training

The AS *mouth-with-no-filter* was well-oiled and functioning in the academy. One of the six military veterans in our class, Tony, an expert shooter, announced he would ultimately emerge as the best shot in the class. I couldn't resist. I said, "Not with me in it." This story recounts an instant negative result of *that* Aspie trait.

Now, that's not your normal: *I couldn't resist* cliché. I really couldn't resist. I could hear my brain saying, "Don't do it." but it just came out. Sometimes, I can see it leaving and try to stop it, but it's slippery and gets away. Doctors say we struggle to resist acting on immediate impulses. I didn't struggle; I just let it rip.

The look the other cadet gave me could have killed a goat.

He said, heavy with attitude, "I am an expert shot. I shot expert in the army, and I'll do it here."

I said, "That may be true with a long gun, but we're shooting pistols here; that's a whole 'nother story. I'll bet you I can out-shoot you with a handgun."

His face was a bright purple now, and he muttered, "We'll see."

I love gamesmanship. I had already beaten him.

I knew virtually nothing about guns before I applied to the police department. After I took the test, however, I figured I should probably get up to speed. Aspergers do this with things. I did it with typing, learning the skill at eight years old.

I learned to drive a stick shift by watching my dad from the front seat and probing him with questions while memorizing the sounds of the engine as he shifted.

The most well-known expert on Asperger syndrome writes, *"They have excellent rote memories and become intensely interested in…subjects…They absorb every available fact involving their chosen field…"*[5]

I reached out to my next-door neighbor, who was also a police officer, and asked what kind of gun I should buy for the department.

He said, "You can't carry your own. They issue one."

He added the make and model.

I went to the local gun store and acquired a used one. I found a book given to me by a friend years ago, dusted it off and followed the instructions. Soon, I was consistently on the target, but I wanted to be the best.

The book recommended I buy the *understudy* for the service revolver. The understudy is the exact same gun but shoots a sub-caliber bullet. This let me practice with cheaper ammo.

The entire time at the academy, we fired approximately 500 rounds of ammunition.

There were days I shot that many in a single practice session.

Among the first set of instructions was the warning: *Do not touch these revolvers anywhere but on the range under the supervision of the range personnel.*

On the range, after being issued an actual revolver, we went through several drills we would perform when issued live ammunition. We *dry-fired* through the whole drill to get us used to handling the gun. Dry firing a gun means that the gun is empty. It contains no live ammunition.

[5]Lorna Wing, "Asperger Syndrome: A Clinical Account" (Psychological Medicine, 1981), 120.

Then, live ammunition was issued. We spent the rest of the day shooting bullseye targets at seven and fifteen yards.

A tower occupied by an instructor at the rear of the shooting stations issued orders via loudspeaker:

"Upon completion of this shooting exercise, you will score your targets FROM THE SEVEN YARD LINE and report your scores in order as your target number is called from the tower."

Tony was on *Target # 3*.

I was on *Target # 9*. I exchanged glances with him. He was wearing his war face. He couldn't wait to announce his score.

Each shooter shouted their score to the tower:

Target # 1, eight-seven (87%)

Target # 2, seven-five

Target # 3, nine-seven, accented by a glare in my direction

Target # 4 and so on…

'til

Target # 9, one, zero, zero (100%). I sent Tony a smile.

His eyes looked like something from a cartoon. They bugged out of his head. He couldn't believe it.

Well, he believed it after it repeated itself each day for the rest of the week. In each session, for each target from each distance, on each course, one, zero, zero. It started to get boring.

I practiced; what can I say?

The instructors who originally wanted to change my stance and readjust my shooting position left me alone when they saw my scores. I got accolades instead of corrections.

Except for the head instructor. He didn't like this. How is this kid shooting these scores? Something is wrong.

In the next class, the head instructor said, "Anyone who shoots 100% in this course wins the Distinguished 100 shooting badge. Few possessed this, and no one ever won it while still in the academy."

I said, "Not until now."

He snapped, "We'll see about that."

This comes with the syndrome. I control it better now, but I didn't know I was doing it at that time in my life.

I realized what I just did. I could shoot 200 now, and he would keep me from getting the Distinguished 100 shooting badge.

There were three chances to shoot the 100. The first time, I shot the middle out of the target. Instead of a lot of little holes, there was one big hole in the middle of the chest on the silhouette. Boom! 100%.

He scored my target personally, turned and said, "You passed, but this target does not qualify for the 100%. You get the score for the maximum number of rounds that I can mark on the target."

Would have been nice to know this in advance, but OK, there were more chances to come.

On the second chance, I shot this target like it was a punch card. I put a smiley face on it for cheekiness. Nice little holes were all lined up for easy counting. All that was necessary now was to make the count and give me my badge.

There were several instructors looking, counting and nodding, giving me the wink. My new friend showed up. He made the count and agreed there was the requisite number of holes in the target for the 100%, but he tagged it disqualified because, apparently, the cadet to my right, who was struggling to make a seventy out of a series of sub-sixty scores, inadvertently put three of his rounds in the lower right edge of my target.

So, I scored over 100%, therefore disqualified. Joseph Heller would be proud.

There was one more shot, pun intended, but I knew he was not going to let me get it. I did something to save face. I noticed there were several nails holding the target frame together. I also knew there was a certain score for each level of shooting badge.

I decided to shoot the exact score to get the lowest shooting badge, collect one of each, and then shoot the nails out of the frame, holding up the target.

I mentioned this to Tony.

I counted till I was sure I shot the minimum number and took the nails out of the backboard. Crash, down it came.

Ooops.

Man, was he pissed. He was as pale as me, and his face was meltdown-red. I don't know what happened. I guess I missed. I think maybe the guy on Target # 10 shot the target frame. He needs to be more careful.

Some careful counting later and now I have just enough holes in the target for a sharpshooter's badge. But he got me again.

It seems they used to have a marksman's badge. This wasn't in the instructions prior to the course, and no one knew it existed. He did, though. The marksman's badge was one step below the sharpshooter's badge.

He found some and issued them to the folks who shot scores below the sharpshooter's badge. This foiled my plan to collect the entire set and wear them all on my uniform. Once you shot one level, you couldn't shoot for the lower badge.

He got me again. But he was still large and sweaty, and I was svelte and beautiful, and I did shoot the 100% twice in the academy, whether he believed it or not.

Chapter 9

Don't Touch the Guns.

Remember the admonition not to carry a gun while in the academy? I took this seriously. Others, not so much.

This was a clear and literal message to me; the literal part of AS is usually not open for interpretation. That gun was like a red-hot stove to me. I wouldn't even think of touching it while not on the range.

I was in the head when Mike, a friend since high school, went to the urinals, pulled out his gun, clanked it on the tile ledge in front of him and took care of business. Then he snatched the gun up, stuck it in the holster and left. I couldn't have done that.

I was too literal to do that. They said, "Don't touch the guns." That said it all to me. Rules were rules.

When we went on details and field training, the range issued each of us 18 rounds of live ammunition in sealed manila envelopes with the instructions: *"Do not load your gun until you arrive at your details. Or, in the case of field training, until you reach your field training district." "Do not do it!"*

A *detail* is any assignment outside your normal routine. It could be anything: a parade, a crime scene or the Rocky detail. There's a chapter ahead dedicated to *field training*.

I was behind Joe as he exited the academy that afternoon. I almost crashed into him when he stopped in the doorway. I watched, amazed, as he tore open the sealed envelope containing the ammo, loaded his gun with six rounds, stuck the extras in his pocket, threw the envelope on the ground and stuck the gun in his belt.

He looked back, smiled and said, "See ya."

I stood there for a second and looked down. There were dozens of torn envelopes on the ground.

But, for some reason, I still couldn't bring myself to load the thing until I was in the uniform, but I did do it before I got to the details.

I was OK with the first part of the instructions, but I wasn't going to drive to a detail in a full police uniform with an unloaded gun.

Chapter 10

An Important New Friend

I was disappointed with the *leather gear* or *rig* they issued in the academy. Leather gear consists of the Sam Browne Belt, the big belt worn on the outside of the uniform, the gun holster, a garrison belt to hold up your pants and the loop for the stick. Unencumbered by the social norm of *accept-it-and-shut-up*, I set out to fix the situation.

The first thing I did was upgrade the holster, which may have been *state of the art* for 1950, but in 1977 was state of the *Ark*. I checked the rules. They were silent on upgrading leather equipment.

My friend in the gun store was a retired police officer. He was excited about me being in the academy and said, "Let me see your badge."

He said, "I know the guy who wore it before you. He went out on disability."

I filed the information. I found if it happens twice, they retire the badge number.

He turned up his nose at the issued holster and said, "Come in back."

He replaced the city holster with a more contemporary design.

He also threw in two slap jacks, flat blackjacks, that were more comfortable sitting on in the police car. One was a normal size, but the other read "Big John" and was about a foot long.

He said, "This is for when you go to Highway Patrol. You stick it in your boot."

I couldn't imagine an immediate use for Big John, but I thanked him and gathered up my loot.

I found the new holster much more serviceable than the issued one and carried it until I was able to identify the ultimate design some months later. All the information for the upgrades came from the same book or from the same authors of the book that taught me to shoot.

During a lull in training one day, I was in a common corridor when I noticed cadets casually talking. I joined the conversation, without invitation, a common mistake of mine, and I got strange looks. I learned later how to judge whether to join a conversation, but at this time, I was still at the mercy of *no-mirror-neurons*[6].

The commandant walked past, stopped, turned around and came back.

He approached me and said, "Why is your handcuff case upside down?"

I said, "I can get them out faster, watch."

I turned and demonstrated how fast they fell into my hand.

He said, "Interesting." and continued to his office.

I could feel one set of eyes on me and turned to see one of the larger members of my class. I met his eyes and stared at him. Another bad habit I've been able to remediate. One doctor writes we do this, *"...searching for the meaning that eludes him."*[7] you know, no mirror neurons.

A thought suddenly hit me, I said, "I have something for you."

I would often, at this point in my life, *assume* everyone knew me.

He looked at me like I was crazy and said, "What?"

---

[6] A mirror neuron is a neuron that fires both when an action is performed and when you see someone do the same action. This allows babies to imitate other humans they see, practicing and learning new skills. It also causes us to feel emotions when we see other people experiencing them.
National Library of Medicine - National Center for Biotechnology Information
https://www.ncbi.nlm.nih.gov/pmc/articles/PMC3898692/#:~:text=Mirror%20neurons%20are%20a%20class,act%20performed%20by%20another%20individual.

[7] Asperger syndrome: a clinical account - Lorna Wing, from the MRC Social Psychiatry Unit, Institute of Psychiatry, London, February 1981.

I said, "I'll bring it in tomorrow."

Again, the weird looks.

The next morning, I brought the Long John to class. The next time I saw this cadet, I greeted him and handed him the jack.

I said, "This is way too big for me. It's just the right size for you."

He took the slap-jack and smiled, but he still wasn't sure what I was all about.

He introduced himself as Barry.

I learned later that he asked around about me to find out what I was all about.

He got the rapidly becoming common, "Oh, that's just Cubbage. That's the way he is."

Barry played football for Cheney State while working on his degree prior to entering the academy.

He approached me the next day, and we chatted for a while.

He announced, "We're going to work together when we get out of here."

I liked the idea but was skeptical, wondering how he could know that.

He was in big demand. Vice, narcotics and several outside agencies wanted him. He told me later he declined all those offers because he wanted to stay in the city, and the other units were not good for someone who wanted a family.

I filed away the thought of working with him but thought it was just banter. I mean, how would he do that? How would he even know where we were going to end up? The chance we would be in the same district with a sergeant who would let two rookies work together was a non-starter.

There was no way for me to know at the time, but something was afoot. I see the signs in retrospect, but I was a naive kid caught up in the excitement.

Barry knew. His comment about working together was a tell I missed at the time but can see now. He obviously possessed more information than I did. Something clearer in 20/15 hindsight.

Chapter 11

Field Training

I don't know how I survived Field Training. I don't mean it was scary or anything. I entered an environment with strict paradigms with my performance closely observed, and at twenty-three, I was anything but malleable.

To better prepare us for the street, we trained our third month in working police districts. We donned real police uniforms, the same ones the police officers wore, and left the academy to train with them under the direct supervision of corporals, sergeants and lieutenants.

I constantly monitored myself in my interactions with the supervisors lest I step on my poncho with *my* usual behavior, which was anything but normal.

I would spend the next month working through all three shifts:

- *Midnight to Eight* - AKA *Last-Out*: I'll call this *Midnights* throughout the book,

- *Four to 12* - AKA *Nights:* We'll call this *Night Work,*

- *Eight to Four* - AKA *Days:* Just *Days.*

AKA = Also Known As.

Shifts rotated from Midnights to Night Work to Days. We worked six days in a row and then took two days off.

Field training was the best part of the academy. It was the third month, just after the pistol range. I rotated among the supervisors, who evaluated me and sent reports to the academy.

I drew the 16th District, located at 39th Street and Lancaster Avenue in West Philly. I told my cop friends.

They said, "What did you do to deserve that?"

Apparently, the 16th was one of the most, if not *the* most, economically depressed areas of the city. There was a saying that all the victims of the 16th were in adjoining districts because there was nothing of value *in* the 16th. This meant robbers and burglars who lived in the 16th, went to adjoining districts to commit their crimes. Then ran back into the 16th.

As was my usual habit, I did a drive-by to see the lay of the land before reporting for duty. What a dump.

The I in the word POLICE over the front door leaned against the C. The step into the building, initially white marble, was now black with city crud; I didn't want my shoes to touch it.

A large overgrown tree hid most of the façade, obscuring the once illuminated, now dead electric sign on the corner, originally meant to act as a beacon when this was a viable neighborhood.

I drove by twenty years later, and it was still that way.

I reported for duty to a squad who were on midnights. I arrived in the middle of the tour, so we did four days of midnights, took two days off, returning for night work. I presented myself to the corporal.

The academy staff warned us to avoid anything *serious* during field training. It could interrupt our progress and delay our graduation.

Serious meant, *Don't arrest anyone,* and, whatever you do, *Don't shoot anyone.*

Well, I didn't shoot anyone. I got it half-right.

The first week burst with excitement, with me making my first felony *pinch*, cop talk for *arrest*, what I call *The Peasant Story*.

Chapter 12

Supervisors

There are special units in each police district, but the bulk of the personnel are street cops. These are the folks who respond when you call 911. They comprise the four squads of officers who complement the district. They do the Police Work.

There are two squads – *A* and *B* – run by sergeants. *A* squad comes in ½ hour before *B* squad, so there is an overlap at shift change, and there are always patrol cars on the streets.

Sergeants report to a lieutenant. Lieutenants act as tie-breakers if the sergeants can't agree on something. In most squads, the lieutenant stays in the background.

In each district there is an operations room, an office staffed by police officers processing the paperwork generated by the street cops. They also keep track of attendance and other data. A corporal supervises the operations room. They are *the inside crew*.

I took turns working with each of the supervisors so they could evaluate my performance and prepare evaluations to add to my overall grade.

Chapter 13

Noodge Me, Nudge You

Hazing started almost as soon as I entered the 16th and ended just as abruptly. Hazing Aspies is ill-advised.

People think the police shift starts at roll call. That's the official start, but among cops, it starts in the locker room. I worked out of the trunk of my car, so I never saw the inside of the 16th's locker room, where rookies on-field training must have been a topic.

Since I was not a member of the district but a cadet still assigned to the academy, I went directly to the operations room. The corporal told me to wait in the roll call room. The roll call room is the central or main room in every district headquarters building. Police officers line up for inspection, briefings, and assignments at the beginning of each shift in this central room.

In the district that serves as divisional headquarters, the roll call room also serves as a courtroom.

When several police officers started to come into the room and loosely form ranks, I went and stood among them. I got the expected looks, and some asked if I was from the academy.

As the time approached for the start of the roll call, a group of police officers emerged from the locker room. They approached the group already forming, and one came directly at me and proclaimed, "You're in my spot!"

I moved over a spot, half expecting the next one to do the same, but they let me stay, watching the one who chased me. He stood directly to my right, breathing heavily and staring. I could see something was up;

the others were looking at us. They knew something was about to happen. But they didn't know *me*.

I've always liked a good staring contest because I usually win. Something about the combination of the *flat affect*, unusual eye color, immunity to social norms and, most importantly, the ability to keep quiet.

I stood and stared back at my new friend until he said, "You want to see a trick? Watch this."

With that, this rocket surgeon pulled out his service revolver and stuck it in his own mouth. As the others looked on, he said, as well as anyone can with a gun barrel in their mouth, "There. How do you like that? What do you think of that?"

As he got as close to me as he could with a crazy look on his face, I could see the other police officers looking on to see what I would do, and when he was close enough to touch, I leaned and nudged him away with my shoulder.

I'm not big for people in my personal space.

I thought he was going to shit himself. He pulled the gun out of his mouth with such force he almost knocked loose a tooth with the front sight.

He started screaming, "What are you crazy?! Are you nuts?!"

I calmly replied, "I'm not the one with the gun in my mouth."

The other police officers, trying to recover control over their gaped mouths and bug eyes, began to laugh as the sergeant came out of the operations room and ordered, "Ok, line up."

The police officer beside me continued to stare at me throughout the roll call as the others snickered under their breath. When roll call broke my new friend scurried off to find his car and avoided me the rest of my stay.

Someone commented, "You're alright, kid. It's about time someone put him in his place."

Some years later, I ran into some of the guys from the 16th who recounted the story to others as a war story adding for some reason, he stopped practicing *his trick*.

Chapter 14

That's My Peasant.

"Curiouser and curiouser!"

— Alice in Alice's Adventures in Wonderland by Lewis Carroll

The first night with the lieutenant was a real eye-opener. It was rumored that he worked for some clandestine governmental agency, and this was his day job. He loved action, carnage and gunplay.

He talked out of the side of his mouth in mumbles. He gave the impression he was pointing his mouth to the side like a directional speaker, so he didn't have to turn and could keep his eyes directed ahead. Something a person frequently in dangerous situations would do.

His physique and body language was that of a Tim Burton cartoon character.

He came to roll call and said, "Oh good, drivers."

When we got to his car, *16 DC,* he said, "How long have you had your driver's license?"

I said, "Since high school, about six years."

He said, "Good, you drive. The last cadet from the academy got her license for the job. I had to drive the whole time."

I quickly absorbed the chatter coming from the police radio, starting with the car numbers. All patrol cars in a district begin with that district's number. In this case, 16.

The lieutenant, the highest rank in each squad, was 16-Command. His car wore the number 16 DC. When the dispatcher wanted him, they would call *"Sixteen Command."* The lieutenant answered, *"Sixteen Command."*

The sergeants of A and B squads were *"Sixteen-A-Andy"* and *"Sixteen-B-Barney"*, respectively.

The patrol car officers responded to their car numbers starting with 163, which the dispatcher would call *"One Six Three"* and so on, until they reached 1610, called *"Sixteen-Ten"*, then *"Sixteen-Eleven"*, etc.

The wagons all carried two officers. Their numbers were the hundreds, starting with "Sixteen Hundred", progressing through *"Sixteen-Oh-One"*, *"Sixteen-Oh-Two"*, and so on.

I was surprised to find the talk over the radio, from the dispatcher to the cars and from the cars to the dispatcher, was plain English. Dispatchers and officers used few codes. The exceptions were *1037* for a drunk driver, the shortened *DK* for drunk, and *5292* for a dead body. Everything else was in plain English.

If the officer encountered someone they thought demented, they were simply a *demented person*. Anyone who called the police or were a victim were simply *the complainant or the hospital case*.

Oh, another thing: police officers acknowledged every call from the dispatcher with, *"OK"*.

Not *Roger*, or *10-4*, or any of that nonsense you see on T.V.

Somehow, for Philly, it seemed curiously appropriate.

There was lots of jargon cop talk, which I'll explain as we go, but everything was out in the open. One example is when officers spoke about anything relating to the radio; it was simply *radio*. If they were talking about the dispatcher, they were *radio*. If a message came to you, it was from *radio*. When we spoke to the dispatchers, we called them *radio*.

As in, *"16 DC to radio."* -or- *"Radio, I have a car stopped."*

At about three in the morning the lieutenant and I were driving by the Philadelphia Zoo, the only going concern in the district. The lieutenant brought up the topic of not-too-infrequent calls to the zoo about a *baby crying*, adding at least once a month, the radio dispatcher sent a car to investigate. I pulled up and stopped outside.

He was explaining the *crying baby* was one of the primates inside the zoo that makes a sound like a human baby, and passers-by often called the police to report it.

I was watching him like I used to watch my grandfather when he paused, and a mocking smile drew itself across his face. From the corner of his mouth oozed, "Hmm, look at this character. I wonder what he thinks he's doing."

I followed his gaze to see a man walking toward us. Although slightly wobbly, he walked with determination. He held a *peacock* under his right arm.

You read that right, a peacock!

When the headlights hit the luminescent blue-green body, my brain went on tilt. The bird glowed in three dimensions against the night's gray flatness.

I was now seeing part of the world differently. Not just the gloomy edges of West Philly but the way it changed at night. Everything was different. The way the street lights played on the peacock's feathers in the absence of sunlight made it three-dimensional against a flat background.

The oppressive, humid air of the daylight hours was fleeing a cooler, heavier air flowing into the void. As the man approached, it was as if he was swirling through this heavy night air.

The man grew large as he came close with this treasure under his arm like a brown-paper-bagged six-pack.

The lieutenant said, "Hmmmmm…. I think we better have a talk with this gentleman."

His eerie way of speaking gave pause to what he was going to do next. We got out and hit the sidewalk as the man reached our car.

The lieutenant said, "Excuse me, sir. What are you doing?"

The man replied, "I'm going home." (I love the literal.)

The lieutenant said, "Sir, that bird belongs to the zoo; I'm going to have to ask you to turn it over to us."

The man stopped, backed up a little, and looked at us like we were crazy.

He said, "No, this is my peasant."

That's not a typo; he said *peasant*.

Now, the lieutenant and I knew he meant pheasant, so we disregarded the assault on the Queen's and the lieutenant tried again.

"Sir, that's not a pheasant; it's a peacock. It's a rather expensive bird that belongs to the Zoo."

The man backed up a little further and strengthened his position, "It's my peasant. I caught it, and I'm taking it home to cook it."

The lieutenant and I looked at each other. I wasn't on the street a week and was already collecting my first *If-I-hadn't-seen-it-myself* story.

The lieutenant tried a different tack.

He said, "Sir, that's not a pheasant; it's a peacock. It's a $2,000 bird that belongs to the zoo. They occasionally jump over the zoo's wall and walk around on the outside. I can understand you think you've caught something good, but it doesn't belong to you, and I'm going to have to ask you again to give it to us so we can return it to the zoo."

The peasant man wasn't having it. He waved his free hand and blasted us his thoughts in a spirit-scented cloud. His thoughts were: *We were trying to steal his dinner.*

All the while, the peasant, I mean peacock, was calmly watching the action. This exchange was not ruffling *his* feathers. Accustomed to humans, none of this bothered him, and a class of school boys on a field trip wasn't chasing him, so he was enjoying a calm evening, watching the show.

The lieutenant motioned to me to flank the man as he moved toward him.

He said, "Sir, the peacock belongs to the Philadelphia Zoo; we're going to have to take it."

He added, "We can do this the easy way or the hard way; it's up to you, but we *are* taking it."

"You can either give it to us and walk on, or you can make it difficult and go to jail."

He chose the hard way, planted his feet, and reinforced his grip on the bird. The lieutenant reached over and grabbed him by his right arm. I grabbed him from the other side.

The lieutenant said, "Last chance."

He didn't budge. He would not relinquish the bird.

With a nod from the lieutenant, we pulled his arms simultaneously. The peacock extended his wings and glided to a landing on the lawn by the front gate. The lieutenant and I met at the man's back, and before he could react, I handcuffed him.

We walked him to the back of 16 DC, and I performed a frisk. As proof, there was little of value in the 16th, he carried nothing on him other than his house key and ID.

The lieutenant radioed for a wagon as I guarded the prisoner. The man voiced how wrong it was, we were stealing his peasant. He caught it fair and needed it for his dinner. No amount of explaining could convince him his pheasant was an exotic bird from the zoo.

I gathered although he lived a few blocks from the oldest and most famous zoo in the country, he had never been inside, never seen a peacock.

When I asked him if he had ever seen a pheasant before, he said on his grandfather's farm. I asked if he had ever seen one so big or easy to catch. He explained this was a city-peasant, so it was bigger, and since it was big, it was slow.

I tried to explain what a peacock was; it was an exotic African bird, and it was worth a lot of money, but he still didn't get it, nor did he believe me.

I told him it would be better to rethink his position. He should convince the lieutenant he made a mistake or he was facing felony REAP (which is how we referred to receiving stolen property) at the least and possibly felony theft at the worst.

I created a new and different problem.

The man started screaming, "I can stand the theft charge, but you ain't putting no rape charge on me. I didn't rape no one!"

I said, "No, not rape, REAP."

"REAP, rape, I didn't do none of that," he shouted.

I guess I should have learned from the un-peasant outset that reasoning with this man was a lost cause. The commotion brought the lieutenant and the newly arrived wagon crew running.

"What's the matter now?" the lieutenant said.

I started to explain what happened, resulting in peals of laughter.

"I never heard that one before." said one of the wagon crew.

"I didn't do no REAP." jested his partner.

Shoulders bouncing with laughter, they led the peasant man to the wagon.

The lieutenant motioned to the peacock and said, "Let's go to the gate."

At the front gate was a lighted doorbell button marked Security. Within minutes, a guard opened the gate.

He said, "What can I do for you, gentlemen?"

The lieutenant told him our peacock tale as the peacock calmly walked around the lawn hunting bugs. The guard, obviously a veteran peacock wrangler, calmly shooed the peacock toward the gate. The peacock gave him an indignant look and scooted through the open gate into familiar darkness.

The lieutenant asked if he wanted to press charges against the peasant man. In between fits of laughter, he said, "It would almost be worth it to hear him tell story in court," but he said, if it was all the same, he was just as happy to have the peacock back inside the zoo.

We thanked him and left.

Back inside the car, the lieutenant asked me what I learned from all this. I admitted to being confused. No matter what we did, we could not convince the man the peacock was not a pheasant he had fairly caught and was going to eat.

I was incredulous anyone would confuse the two, let alone go home with a 40-pound bird with the intention of killing, preparing and eating it.

And the REAP thing, what was that all about?

The lieutenant got his wry smile on, and out of the side of his mouth came, "Welcome to Powelton Village. The best is yet to come. Here, you'll hear the language butchered like nowhere else, and it's heard as wrong as it's said."

He elaborated, "He never heard the acronym REAP before, but he's heard the word rape. Since It's coming from the police, he heard the word he's familiar with. If you explained it, his head would have exploded when you got to the word *acronym*."

He added, "Introducing a word like *acronym* to progress from peasant to pheasant to peacock would have been way too complicated."

He said, "You did good, though, and under different circumstances, you would have come away with your first felony arrest, but I'm sure you can see the wisdom of handling this as what it was: a case that doesn't belong in the criminal justice system."

I could see that. He wasn't a criminal, but a bumpkin applying grandpop's out-of-synch farm lessons to inner-city life, and who was as badly out-of-synch with peasants, pheasants and peacocks as I was in his world of inner-city-peasant barbeques.

After a firm lecture about staying away from the flora, fauna and pheasants of the zoo, he got a berth for the night to excise the spirits.

He was lucky, though; he met the 4:00 AM cut-off for breakfast.

Thank God a hippo hadn't escaped from the zoo. Consider the size of that pig roast.

Chapter 15

I Don't Need Another Baby

I started to see the jading process trying to work on me early on when one night, the Lieutenant and I responded to a *report of a rape at the Presbyterian Hospital ER.*

Presbyterian Hospital at that time was like something out of *12 Monkeys.* Philadelphia was perfect for that movie. The properties suitably dilapidated and film-ready as post-apocalyptic locations.

The Lieutenant told me to respond for two reasons. One, he wanted to expose me to as many different types of calls as possible, and two, he was interested in anything that involved carnage, violence or mayhem.

The dispatchers broadcast crimes as *in progress* or *report-of.* A crime *in progress* was happening now. It got a rapid response. *Report of* crimes happened in the past, and the victim was calling to report it to the police. We responded quickly but not as we would to an emergency.

A *report of a rape at the Presbyterian Hospital* ER meant the rape occurred someplace else, and the victim was now at the hospital emergency room reporting the crime.

The protocol at this time was to take rape victims directly to an emergency room, so the medical staff could treat any injuries and collect evidence in a rape kit. When we got there the officer who brought the woman to the hospital was with her in the intake cubicle just inside the door to the ER.

The woman was about forty years old, emaciated and loud. She was answering questions from the intake receptionist, providing her name, date of birth, address, etc. She didn't have insurance. Insurance was rarer then than it is now. I can't remember a single instance where someone I took to an inner-city emergency room produced an insurance card.

Suddenly, the woman shouted, "Look, I ain't got time for all this. Just get this stuff out of me. I don't need another baby."

The lieutenant said, "Hmmmmm. Quite the lady, huh?"

The atmosphere in this part of the city was a stark contrast to where I grew up. A permanent dimness permeated every crevice of the place. It was palpable; you could feel it around and above you like a cloud of some eerie substance.

The district's reputation was as a dumping ground. As a refuge to some, rejected from other assignments. I don't know if this was true, but it was certainly gloomy. Some officers wore the same look as the inhabitants. A kind of resigned, sad, abandoned look.

It felt as though the whole place was dying.

Chapter 16

A Petunia in an Onion Patch

The Lieutenant, along with his other quirks, liked hospital cafeterias. I know what stigma is associated with this idea, but when your mom is Irish, and you can tell the day of the week by what's on the dinner table, variety is good.

Add to the fact I was a frequent visitor to hospitals growing up, either as a patient or visitor, I didn't have negative paradigms about the place and, especially about the food. Years of exposure to finer foods in the interim have provided me with an education and point of comparison, however, so I get the whole *hospital food = nasty* idea.

But, in 1977, in a place with food limited to either what you brought yourself or what the locals ate, the hospital was more than acceptable.

The lieutenant ate like a bird. He recognized other folks' need to eat, however, so he got a coffee, found a seat and waited while I walked through the café line.

It was the usual set-up with a stack of orange trays beside the silverware and napkins. Plasticware wasn't in vogue yet, so it was metal forks and knives.

I perused the cuisine and settled on a hamburger and two containers of milk. I unknowingly set the stage for something.

I took my place in the cashier's line behind two nurses. Nurses were easy to spot at this time in their white uniforms, caps and white shoes. These were busy chatting.

Sheldon says about peripheral vision, "On a good day, I can see my ears."[8] It's sometimes hard to explain to normal folks what this is like.

As I'm standing in line, I'm monitoring the chatter, the ambient noises, the kitchen sounds, the trays struck by metal utensils, clanking and sliding on the stainless-steel rail/shelves in front of the food on display behind the glass.

I can hear each separate conversation in the booths, behind the counter, in the line, in the kitchen and at the register. I detailed this phenomenon in my first book when it first surfaced in grammar school.

When this happens, it often looks like I've zoned out. If I'm people-watching, my favorite thing, I'm scanning and watching, but if I focus on something, people think I've lost touch. What I'm doing is ignoring them.

I'm seeing everything, hearing everything. My brain is processing and storing. If something important shows up, I'll focus on the issue. If my brain doesn't perceive anything important, the scanning continues.

As I stood in line this evening, I fixed my eyes on the hair of the nurse in front of me, the one facing away. Not like one would focus on repairing a watch but focused on the image of the hair. It attracted my attention because it stood out.

It was a break in a pattern; it was different.

I never saw hair this shiny. It was chestnut brown, which is a color I'd seen many times, but the sheen added a different dimension. The color was more vivid, more vibrant and radiated depth.

Its shininess drew me in, and since no one can stare like an Aspie, I fixated as I awaited my turn to pay.

---

[8] Jim Parsons: Sheldon Cooper
https://www.imdb.com/title/tt3823254/characters/nm1433588

As the owner of the hair continued to chatter, the other nurse, who was facing my direction, edging backward toward the cashier, caught me staring. At first, she just looked, figuring I would notice her glare and stop. I could see her in my periphery, but lacking the requisite social firmware, I continued to focus on the back of the other nurse's head.

When the nurse facing attempted eye contact (Good luck with that!), she did so over the head of shiny hair. Not because she was particularly tall but because the other was *très petite*. She simply looked up from their conversation, directly at me.

She stared for a few seconds while the other nurse continued to chatter-on until she realized I wasn't paying attention to her. She felt she had given me enough warning, so she looked back at her friend, made eye contact and nudged her eyes in my direction, communicating non-verbally, "Look behind you."

The other nurse stopped talking momentarily, turned and looked up at me.

When she did this, I fell out of character. Normally, I have a completely flat affect. I can maintain this through disasters, autopsies, sad movies, almost anything.

But when I saw her face, my jaw dropped.

Picture a countenance that the Hümmel factory would like to stamp on every figurine they ever made. Under the shiny chestnut hair was an exquisite face. Rosy cheeks complemented perfect skin and cobalt blue eyes that could turn sapphires green.

When she smiled, I couldn't feel my legs.

She took a quick scan of the tray I was holding, looked at the milk, laughed and turned back to her friend.

By the time the world stopped spinning, she and her friend were gone.

I snapped out of it when the "*Ahem.*" hit me from behind.

47

I hurried through the cashier and looked around the place, figuring they were in a booth. They were gone. I started into the corridor when the lieutenant firmly reminded me, he was waiting for me in a nearby booth.

I sat down and looked at him.

He said, "I saw that. That's another good reason to eat here."

I spent the balance of the month in and around the hospital looking for that nurse. On other visits, I questioned the nurses, but the idea of a uniformed police officer looking for a nurse was not something new. They were not going to tell me who she was even if they did know.

And I couldn't escalate the search. I'm not a stalker. Aside from the occasional *casual* drive-by on the way home and keen attention to my surroundings on subsequent duty-related visits to the hospital, there was nowhere else to go.

Not understanding the idea of the social network, the manual one in place at the time, not the one in place on the web now, I was on my own.

I didn't understand networking. If I did, I might have had some luck, but at the end of the month, I was back at the academy, and any idea of drive-bys or visits to this hospital, which was out of the way, would have to wait.

Chapter 17

50 First Dates

There was an Adam Sandler movie in the early 2000s in which a man went on fifty-first dates with the same woman. Her memory, which lasted only twenty-four hours, meant he was meeting her for the first time each day for 50 days. Critics tag the film a *psychological romantic comedy*. I don't know about you, but that sounds scary to me.

The man tries to win the woman's love each new day. Since she wakes each day with no memory of the past, he has his work cut out for him.

God works in mysterious ways. He was about to put the whole dating idea on ice for me.

The experience also awakened me to perceptions held by some people about my new career choice.

I feel like I'd been on fifty-first dates but with different women. That's an exaggeration, but not much. And I have to say, most of it was on me.

There were a few who I would have liked to re-date who declined to return calls, but 99% of it was me being too *selective*. A psych would say, "*Pedantic.*" Both flowery words for *picky*.

As much as there was a selection process happening on their side of the table, unbeknownst to them, there was an even more stringent one on my side. A lot of it seemed to center around symmetry. I've since learned this is a *normal* tendency in humans; seeking symmetry one of the few things I do that is.

I took it to another level.

Are their eyes too far apart, their nose too big, their ears too far away from their head? In summary: Do they resemble someone who was purpose-built or someone built from spare parts?

Once they passed the initial physical symmetry filter, others surfaced. Are they compatible with me socially, culturally, religiously, morally, and ethically? Do they have an acceptable temperament, are they empathetic, to name a few.

Psychologists call this *assortative attraction* or *assortative mating*. I went beyond that.

I was looking for someone as a partner. Not a sexual partner, per se, as it seemed most of my contemporaries were, but a match, mate, or dovetail with me.

Combining all this was a monumental task. For a visual of this, an analogy, look at pictures of *recording studio equalizers and digital mixers.*

Your mission is getting them to match.

And remember, I'm looking for a match to someone who is in a group of 0.026% of the population. When you do the math, don't forget the %. There are about one million possible candidates for me to choose from, or about eight billion fewer than normal folks.

To get the math to tie, remember I'm looking for women, so cut the numbers in half.

I thought I was operating with a sound, logical system. Sometimes, my system caused situations like the next one.

Chapter 18

Preemptive Irish Exit

I love learning something new. In this instance, I learned and taught it in the same instance.

I met a young woman while I was still in the academy. She worked in a candy store in center city. She pointed out that this was a part-time job. Her normal Monday to Friday job was working in an office nearby.

She was working the extra job to pay off an overflowing credit card she was wrestling with as part of her clothing fascination, clearly illustrated by her amazing wardrobe.

She was trying to keep pace with the other women in the office by buying more and more expensive outfits, which led to many outfits, so she did not come to work in any memorable time period wearing the same one. Something impossible to achieve among women in an office setting unless one possesses over 250.

Woman's collective ability to remember what one wears is amazing and baffling.

I found later while working in an office setting, women on the extremes of the attraction/symmetry continuum were less likely to be concerned with this obsession to never wear the same thing twice.

I saw every permutation of this behavior. There were women on the low side of the attraction continuum who dressed to the nines, labeled by others as *pathetic*.

There were those on the extreme upper end of the continuum who dressed to the nines, labeled by others as *pompous*.

Some who were on the high side of attraction who dressed badly, labeled as: *matronly*.

Some were on the low side of attraction and dressed badly, labeled as: *just-plain-nasty*.

Surprisingly, the ones in the middle on most continuums labeled: non-threatening, ergo, OK.

Note: I got these labels from women.

On the high side of the confidence continuum, there were women who would dress in outfits I could tell the day of the week from, yet since they were also high on the personal pride side of the continuum, their outfits were impeccably clean, neat and ironed.

And, since they were high on the other traits, the remarks of the other women rolled like water off a duck.

Which pissed the other woman off.

The one I met in the sweets shop was beyond the high side of the continuum in attraction and symmetry. With hair the color and texture of corn silk, blue eyes the color of Michigan mints, and porcelain skin, she was tall, slim and athletically shapely as if formed in a time and place with no law of gravity.

Top that with the designer clothing, and she was way off the charts.

We enjoyed a nice dinner and spent time walking and talking in center city. I found it was much better to listen than to talk during dates, so when she said, "I hear you're in Temple University. What are you studying?"

I said, "Accounting," and shut up.

She took it from there, talking about accountants in her office and how it seemed like a good career. I didn't correct her.

She aced our first date. Apparently, I did OK, and she agreed to a second.

The second date was dinner and the theatre. Philly enjoyed a robust artistic life with several beautiful theatres staging Broadway shows. I bought tickets to the Shubert.

I picked her up and took two bouquets of flowers, one for her and one for her mom. She told me during our first date her dad died some years ago, so I thought Mom might enjoy some flowers.

Gamesmanship is not just for sports. It never hurts to score points with Mom.

We set off for dinner.

When she got in the car, she said, "What are you going to do after college?"

I said, "I'm in the police academy…" that's all I got out.

She turned and said, "You're not thinking about becoming a cop, are you?!"

I said, "Yes, why?"

She reeled on me with a nasty look and said, "I'll *never* marry a cop!"

She launched into a rant about the nature of cops and that she once dated one who turned out to be married, etcetera, etcetera, ad nauseam.

I couldn't believe someone could go off quite as militantly on a subject like this. It was obviously not a casual dislike but a visceral disgust with the whole idea.

The married guy poisoned her to everyone.

I was also processing the *marriage* remark with mixed feelings. In one sense, we were both thinking along the same lines, finding a partner, but it seemed *kind* of premature after only one date.

I know I'm a catch, but really.

She ranted and raved for three blocks. I tried to get a word in, but she wasn't having it. I listened during the three blocks, which can be several minutes in this part of Philly, with the composure expected of a gentleman.

I watched the sliders on those non-physical continua gradually move from neutral to the bottom. The more she talked, the more they slid. It took a lot to cancel out this level of beauty, but she was working overtime.

I tell a story in my first book about another woman's negative reaction to my career choices. When that woman declared me persona non grata, she showed the grace to do it over the phone, saving me gas, time, and money.

This one was blasting me about my chosen career and labelling me an ineligible life partner while enjoying a night out at my expense.

She wanted me to sit on my hands and *pay* for insults.

I drove on, and she continued to rant. I turned right, and right again, and right once more.

Absorbed in her tirade, we were sitting back in front of her house for a full minute before she realized.

She paused, like jamming on the brakes, and glanced around with a startled and confused look.

She said, "Why are we back at my house?"

I reached over, opened her door and flatly said, "Get out." abandoning Mom's rule to always get out to open the door for a lady.

It took a second for her to get it, but she finally collected herself and her crap and got out.

When she did, I reached over and pulled the door shut.

I could hear her saying something through the window and see her staring in amazement through the rearview mirror as I drove off, but that was the end of that.

She breached a threshold, an Aspie thing. The fact she would not even let me get a word in displayed an insurmountable level of intolerance.

There were two *positive* outcomes:

1. I found out before it was too late,

2. I found a new application of the *Irish Exit.*

I wasn't above dinner and the theater solo. As I passed the line at the box office I said, "Anyone need a ticket?"

I passed it off to another solo patron, an elderly woman. We enjoyed the show and each other's company without drama or baggage.

We did enjoy a laugh, though, when she said, "Why are you here alone?" and I told her the story.

At first her eyes bugged, but she recovered fast and said, "Serves her right."

I couldn't agree more.

Chapter 19

Siren-head,
Another almost Pinch

You never know what you'll find when you meet a stranger on a dark Philly street at two in the morning.

We came from the academy with a checklist. Among the requirements for the supervisors to check off were *activity*. Activity consisted of traffic tickets, car stops, and pedestrian or ped stops. Some supervisors counted *part-one* and *part-two* crimes, felonies and misdemeanors activity as well.

That night, the sergeant was going to introduce me to the fine art of the ped-stop. The reason for these was intel collection and crime prevention. When you saw someone out late at night involved in suspicious activity, you would initiate a conversation.

If warranted, if you felt physically threatened, you might frisk the person.

The sergeant was in the process of explaining all this when *lo and behooweld*[9] a suspicious person walked down the otherwise deserted residential street with a large brown paper bag under his arm.

The sergeant said, "Let's see what this guy has to say."

We got out of the car and approached him. He started to act a little squirrelly, with his eyes darting back and forth between us, and he tried to hide the two-foot-wide paper bag by shifting his body.

---

[9] Philly accent.

He gave his name. The sergeant told him to put the bag on the trunk of the police car.

The sergeant gave the information to the radio dispatcher. The dispatcher replied that the man showed an active warrant. I handcuffed him.

The sergeant said, "See what's in the bag."

In the bag was the siren-head from a police car. The small console for controlling the radio bands and siren frequencies. The thief must have thought the siren-head was a police radio. That part was in the trunk.

He said, "What is it?"

I said, "The siren-head out of a police car."

He said, "Get out of here."

I said, "Take a look." and opened the bag....

Since the academy didn't want us involved, the sergeant turned the pinch over to the wagon crew.

Although I didn't get the pinch, I did get recognition for having discovered the stolen siren-head, and this reached the academy.

The academy instructors collected stories like this and shared them with the class in our final month. This was not the best, but it was among the funniest after the peasant story.

Chapter 20

Figuring out the Stick

People don't like change. I worked with a detective who said to resist change in any form. He insisted if approached with the option of staying home, not working and still receiving my pay, I should resist.

He was extreme, but the spirit in the department was one that did not align well with change.

We came into a department, dominated by military veterans, as predominantly non-veteran. Into a *no-educational-requirement*[10] system, we brought a generally higher level of education, including years of college, degrees and letters.

This threatened the existing establishment and conjured rumors of spies, rats and informers. When I hit field training, everyone was prepared to: *Avoid at all Costs.*

We spent nearly all our time with the supervisors, but when an emergency call was issued, they expected us to respond and engage in the situation alongside the other officers.

This is especially true when the dispatcher broadcasts an *assist* call. This means an officer needs immediate help. Officers may only use the word *assist* over police radio as a call for *immediate* help. When an officer uses the word *assist,* everyone drops what they are doing and runs to their aid with lights and sirens.

The first one I experienced occurred right behind the district headquarters. I was working with the sergeant when the call came out. It

---

[10] During my application process I saw the requirements for the job. The bottom line read; no education required.

was about six in the evening, but still daylight. When I heard the call, I instinctively hit the gas.

The sergeant said, "Ok, take it easy."

He put the lights and siren on and said, "Ok, go, but be careful. We can't help anyone if we have an accident."

I drove carefully but quickly to the location. I could see the fight in the street involving a dozen civilians and seven or eight police officers. I rolled the car up to the edge and got out running.

As I got closer, I could see a man walking up behind an officer with a tire iron in his hand.

I called out, "Hey!"

He turned in my direction. I pointed my gun at him and said, "Drop that crowbar!"

He didn't argue but dropped it right at his feet.

I shouted, "Kick it in the sewer." There were always sewer inlets close by.

He kicked it into the sewer.

When he did this, I holstered the gun and ran into the crowd where several officers struggled with a large man. I could see the eyes of the other officers. They were worried I might see them do something out of line.

This was happening fast, I was running, they were looking at me, the bad guy was kicking them and, as he bit one of them, I snatched my stick out of the ring and hit him right in the middle of the forehead. One of the other officers beamed and said, "You're alright, kid." as he pushed the dazed biter to the ground to handcuff him.

This seemed to throw cold water on the rest of the crowd, and things died down.

The sergeant pulled me by the arm.

He said, "Nice, but they'll handle it from here."

Chapter 21

Communal Stomach Problems

This sergeant considered himself something of a sociologist. He proposed a theory. He took me to the local feeding trough to make his point. He had recently read a study done by a major university indicating the trouble inner-city dwellers were having with their stomachs and hearts was hereditary. He thought it was a lot of crap, and he was going to prove it. He drove to a greasy storefront take-out and stopped. He parked right in front so I could see in the window.

It was on the main avenue. You could go in and order your lunch or dinner from a menu on the wall above the counter. They offered chicken, fish, fries and other delicacies.

He told me to tell him what I saw.

I could see each patron come in the front door, look up at the menu and tell the person behind the counter what they wanted. The person behind the counter took their order, went to the refrigerator, got the makings of their meal, and dropped it all in a large deep-fat fryer.

Chicken, beef, fish, corn, fries, whatever, it went into the deep fat fryer.

Diners emerged from this fine establishment with a brown paper bag.

The sergeant said, "Look at the bottom of the bag."

Leaking through the bottom was the fat from the deep fat fryer.

He said, "Watch what happens next."

Invariably the patrons would go next door to the liquor store. They would emerge with another brown paper bag with a bottle in it.

The sergeant hollered, "See. Look at the shit they eat. That's what's wrong with their stomachs and hearts. There's nothing hereditary about it unless being stupid counts."

He continued the health lecture, adding notes about too much salt, no exercise, and terrible hygiene as he lit his third cigarette in less than an hour.

Chapter 22

Intro to Burglary Teams

Burglary teams were plain-clothes officers who specialized in catching burglars. They proved to be an interesting bunch. This was my baffling intro to this unique type of police officer.

I need to provide some background for the story.

We were issued revolvers, which were all the same brand and type. They all wore a blue finish. In short, they all looked the same.

Our training emphasized that undercover cops, plain-clothes officers, could carry their own firearm if it met certain requirements:

- Be of one of two specified manufacturers,

- Be a six or five-shot revolver, with a blue finish,

- No nickel-plated guns for on-duty carry,

- No automatic pistols for on-duty carry,

- No soft holsters stuck in the waistband, and none without a snap retention system.

Another thing you need to consider for this story is that criminals in a particular area reflect the demographics of the immediate area. They don't usually travel far from home base.

On to the story:

I was working with the sergeant when the dispatcher broadcast a *burglary in progress at the gas station, being committed by two males wearing denim jackets, blue jeans and white sneakers.*

It was warm, so the denim jacket seemed slightly out of place, so it stuck.

The radio call also included a description of the males consistent with the demographics of the area.

The sergeant and I were the first to arrive. Other cars pulled up close behind us as I rolled into the parking lot.

I was the first to the front door, the sergeant right behind me.

The front door was open and there were lights on in the office. As we ran to the front door, I could clearly see the burglar climbing in through the rear window.

He fit the description, right demographic, dressed in a *denim jacket, blue jeans and white sneakers.*

He carried a large, not blue, but *nickel-plated revolver* in his hand. It stood out like a beacon!

I drew my revolver. As I raised it to eye level, the burglar made eye contact, and as his foot hit the floor, his balance was unsteady; he teetered on one foot. As he attempted to keep his balance, the revolver pointed in my direction.

I stopped and assumed a shooting stance with him in my sights when the sergeant shouted, "Don't shoot him; he's a cop!"

Apparently, the local burglary team thought that it would be a good idea to come to the location of the burglary, unannounced and instead of coming to the front door, decided to climb through the rear window.

I write unannounced because plain clothes officers are supposed to notify the dispatcher when they respond to an incident, so the uniformed officers are aware that plain clothes officers are responding.

I rarely saw burglary teams on the street after dark because most burglaries are of residences and occur in the daytime.

So, I'm faced with a male fitting the description of the burglar, dressed *as* the burglar, carrying an *unauthorized non-police firearm, climbing through the rear window* of the burglarized property.

How do you explain to a police cadet the wisdom of this set of actions?

I can tell you one thing that was good about the incident, other than the fact that I didn't shoot him.

A city-wide memo went out the next day instructing every plain clothes unit working a district to present themselves to each roll call so the cadets and other officers knew who they were, and this incident did not repeat itself.

All I could think was, "How stupid can one man be?"

Until his partner appeared, wearing a *denim jacket, blue jeans and white sneakers*, with an *automatic pistol stuck in his waistband*.

Chapter 23

The Chief

"I never met a man I didn't like."

— *Will Rogers*

I never wanted to work inside. I thought that would be boring. This night knocked the bottom out of that theory in a hurry.

One night of midnights, I worked inside to learn how an operations room worked.

The corporal said, "Go over, get that big manual, and learn how to use the computer."

"OK," I answered.

He added, "Come and get me if anything happens."

I acknowledged. It felt good; they trusted me now.

Soon, I was alone in the operations room. The district was particularly quiet, *dead* in many ways. The reason I was alone was a poker game in the JAD room.

The Juvenile Aid Division, or JAD, was a unit who handled crimes involving anyone under eighteen years of age. Plain-clothes police officers investigated these crimes. One per division. They conducted interviews and interrogations in an office which opened to the roll call room.

The JAD room was perfect for poker with a table, chairs and a locked door.

That night, in the operations room, I got my first computer experience. Experience that would develop into skills taking me far in the department and beyond. It was me, a dumb terminal and a manual as big as a phone book, you know, as thick as a half-dozen computer tablets piled on top of one another.

Dumb terminals were the first computer terminals in offices at the user level.

I'm getting along fine with the computer when in walks a police officer. He's in to drop off a report. This is routine, as they don't want to overwhelm the inside crew with paperwork at the end of the shift, so they drop them off during the shift to meter the flow.

He was the only one who came in, though, because it was so quiet and little activity meant few reports.

He looked around and said, "Where is everyone?"

"JAD room," I replied.

He nodded knowingly.

Then it happened: the phone rang.

Before I could move, he picked it up.

"Hello?" he said.

Suddenly and violently, he pulled the receiver away from his ear. I could hear the voice on the other end of the phone shouting. I could hear it from across the room.

"*Hello?!*', *'Hello?!'* What the *hell* kind of way is that to answer the phone in a police department?!"

Followed by a litany of excited explanations, exhortations, expletives, threats and other noise.

The officer was alternately looking at the phone, looking at me, pantomiming, and mocking the caller. He was doing the *sock-puppet-*

mouth-thing with his free hand where you satirize someone talking excessively.

He was adding comic faces and all sorts of gestures.

I sat frozen because I knew who it was on the other end of the line.

It was our Chief Inspector.

The chief was a legend in the department. I never got it, but apparently, the street cops didn't like him because he was something of a stickler for the rules. Among other things, he was known for calls and visits to the district during all hours, especially on midnights.

The call rose to a crescendo with, "Do you know who this *is?!*"

The cop looked at me, looked at the phone and calmly said, "No, do you know who *this* is?"

There was a full ten seconds of dead air followed by, "No."

To which the officer replied, "Then, *Fuuuck You.*"

He hung up the phone, calmly walked out of the operations room and left the building.

I sat there frozen for two seconds and then tried to catch up with my feet as they ran to the JAD room, where I hammered on the door.

The door opened a crack; it was the corporal.

I machine-gunned the news of what happened.

"Holy Shit," he shouted. "Everybody out."

I was already back in the operations room when the corporal and the other guys piled in.

"Tell me what happened again." said the corporal.

I recounted the incident.

The corporal ordered everyone into position as he straightened up the operations room. We all settled in to wait. We didn't wait long.

Suddenly, a foot came through the operations room door! No words or knocking, just a foot.

A foot attached to the Chief Inspector. He followed closely behind.

"What the fuck?!" he shouted.

We all tried to look as surprised as we could.

"What the fuck, corporal?" he wailed.

The corporal, unruffled, said, "What's up, Boss?"

The chief screamed, "What's up? What's up? I just called here, and someone told me to fuck myself."

We looked back in disbelief. A look that said the idea someone would do such a thing was foreign to all of us.

The corporal said, "What? Someone here? No, boss. No one here would do that to you."

"As a matter of fact, we've all been sitting here since the start of the shift, and the phone hasn't rung at all all night."

He said it so convincingly the chief paused. He looked at the corporal and at the other officers. He didn't look at me, I was some kid at the computer, probably knew there were cadets out and figured that's who I was.

Anyway, he looked at the corporal and said, "Are you sure?"

The corporal said, "Of course, boss. You know I usually answer the phone and would never answer it that way."

Then the corporal, my hero, said, "Are you sure you dialed the right number?"

The chief froze.

"No," he said. "I could have dialed the wrong number."

Keep in mind there was no caller ID or any way to know where a call came from or where it went in 1977.

The chief's whole demeanor changed.

He said, "You're right, corporal. You're doing a great job. Keep it up."

He turned and was gone.

"Asshole", the corporal muttered under his breath.

I was still bug-eyed for the next few minutes, trying to process all that. But that quick, it was over.

What a weird planet this is.

That was also the end of the poker game for the night.

When I told the sergeant the next evening about this, he shared another interesting story about the chief.

He said the chief told him he wasn't doing a good job, because no one was writing on the men's room walls about him. The chief checked the walls regularly.

I went into the men's room later in the week, and the sergeant was standing on one of the sinks with a magic marker. He was just finishing, "*Will Rogers never met Sergeant X*" written across the wall in big block letters over the sink.

Just before I returned to the academy, I was in the operations room with the sergeant and some other officers when the chief poked his head in the door and said to the sergeant, "You're doing a good job, sergeant. Keep it up."

Chapter 24

Fieldtrips: Super Sunday

The last month in the academy was tedious. We wanted out. They tempered our impatience a bit by taking us on field trips. The first was Super Sunday.

Normal people thrive on gigantic social events, things I avoid like the plague. Philly ran these events called Super-Sunday. There's a large grassy mall in front of the Philadelphia Museum of Art. Much like the area between the Lincoln and Washington Memorials in D.C., sans reflective pond. The city stages Super Sunday events in this area.

We wore real police uniforms now, like real street cops. Our uniform included rain gear, which was a rubber yellow suit with a coat, pants like waders, rubber boots and a cover for the hat.

Thank God they did because it rained on and off all day Super-Sunday.

In the three-block-long swath of Ben Franklin Parkway, there were two blocks dedicated to vendors of food, shirts, art works, collectables and other junk, with still enough room for picnics and games of badminton and kickball.

You could also ride the Merry-Go-Round or snack on cotton candy.

In previous years, the event drew over 300,000 people, the expected turnout until the rain showed up. Despite the rain, however, there were thousands there having fun in the rain and mud and the short intervals of sun. These events were essentially the World's Biggest Block Parties. A Philly tradition.

I was, by the end of the day, despite my yellow duck costume, soaked to the skin. I set my leather gear out to dry and found rust under the grips of my brand-new revolver when I took them off to clean it.

As an Asperger, my assessment was I would have much more enjoyed spending the eight plus hours *inside* the art museum with an apple and a sandwich in a brown paper bag, minus the crowds.

Chapter 25

Fieldtrips: Temple U

Folks tend to enjoy parlor tricks, so here's one for you. We spent a week of our academy training at Temple University, several days with a Professor of Sociology, and half a day with a Spanish-language professor. It was a valuable and revealing week.

I think perhaps a week with a Professor of Psychology might have also been valuable, but that's me. The week with the Sociology Professor was no less valuable.

What I remember about the time with the Sociology Professor was the incessant arguments between him and the class. His theory was our behavior was somehow and largely responsible for the behavior of the people we policed.

I can get behind the idea that in individual interactions, especially violent ones, the behavior of an officer can influence the behavior of others, but the idea we could and would dictate everyone's behavior all the time was not computing.

Nor was it going over well with the class.

One cadet, who happened to be a minister, took offense that the professor would even suggest such a thing. He engaged in constant red-faced arguments with the professor. He also remarked he would never hit another human being and couldn't even contemplate the idea.

There was a book in print at that time called *The Sayings of Chairman Frank*[11]. A parody of *The Sayings of Chairman Mao*. One of the sayings was, "A conservative is a liberal who was mugged the night before."

In the not-too-distant future, shortly after our assignment to the 17th District, I was driving home and passed a group of officers from the nightwork squad. In the middle of the group was our friend, the minister, busy punching someone in the face after the guy punched him.

I guess Chairman Frank was right.

Another salient event in the late 1970s was the newspaper article that surfaced several years after we sat through those sociology lectures at Temple. The article headline on the front page, above the fold, was: "I was wrong. Lock them all up."

The article was a firm refutation of the same professor's theories revealed in an interview of him after he was the victim of a crime. He threw his hands up and said, "I give up. I was wrong. Lock them all up."

So, what's the parlor trick? In the Spanish class, which lasted half a day, we learned the following:

- Soy, policia., I'm the police.

- Tienes armas? Are you armed?

- Tienes cuchillo? Do you have a knife?

- Tienes revolver? Do you have a gun (literally a revolver)? I don't know why he didn't add pistola.

- Cómo te llamas? What is your name?

- Necessita una ambulancia? Do you need an ambulance?

[11] Compilation of Frank Rizzo quotes. Frank Rizzo served as commissioner of the Philadelphia Police Department from 1967 to 1971 and mayor of Philadelphia from 1972 to 1980.

- Déjeme ver su licencia. Give me your license. (Actually, *show* me your license, he taught it as *give*.)

But, for some reason, and notwithstanding the narrow focus of the questions, he taught phonetically. And, for whatever reason, perhaps due to some regional dialect, he taught: Tengo armas? And Como se yama?

So, I was in a class for one day over forty-eight years ago, and those phrases still stick in my head.

When I used this on the street in the company of other officers who were in class with me, they looked at me like I was a wizard.

Ok, that's your eidetic memory demo for this chapter.

Before leaving Temple, the sociology professor gave us a piece of advice that was life-changing for me.

He advised us to "Go and read as many books as you can on *body language.*"

I don't know if anyone else did, but I'm glad I did. As an Asperger, this was a treasure trove of information I would never have even known existed if not for this professor.

It would save me and others on more than one occasion.

And, BTW, The Spanish would be invaluable in case we ever invaded Cuba.

Even after leaving the academy, exposure to other police officers was rare. On one occasion, however, I was in the company of one from another district who was wearing an unusual shirt.

The shirt read: *Phila PD, Cuban Invasion Force.* Apparently, Chairman Frank was at it again. The Cuban Missile Crisis was still fresh in our minds, so this was a typical cop-humor response to something said by a politician.

Cuba today is something we see in the occasional movie, but in the 1970s, those of us who had hidden under our desks in grade school for

Air Raid Drills during the Cuban Missile Crisis still knew it was only 90 miles off the Florida coast and that the Soviet Union, the #2 superpower, was their #1 trading partner.

In an interview, Chairman Frank said, "...we [The Philadelphia Police Department] could invade Cuba and win." Within weeks the *Cuban Invasion Force T-shirts* popped up all over the police department commemorating the interview. The more irreverent an event, the more likely it would appear on a T-shirt or baseball cap.

Chapter 26

Fieldtrips: ME's office

The most memorable field trip was to the medical examiner's office. They split the class into groups of twenty-five so we could walk through in a manageable way. Unlike the ME's offices you see on T.V., the ME's office in Philly was one giant porcelain tiled *room-slash-refrigerator* with rows and rows of stainless-steel rolling tables on which lay the naked bodies of those unfortunates who passed on in the last few days.

I would estimate during our visit, there were 30. (Actually, there were 32, but that's too Aspie-like to remember the exact number.) (I'm not counting the two in the autopsy room.)

I imagine the lesson was introducing us to what it was like to be in the presence of a dead body or something along those lines. Instructors showed us the loading dock where various vehicles loaded and unloaded the bodies passing through the facility.

These vehicles were often police wagons, so they wanted to show us where to bring bodies when we came to the office. While we were there, there were several hearses, not a common term or sight today, picking up bodies to take to funeral homes for final burial.

So, police wagons, rescue vehicles, private ambulances, and hearses from funeral homes would pull into this area to load and unload bodies.

Inside the facility, we walked through the aisle between the rows of bodies. We toured the offices and, finally, the examination room.

The examination room was essentially an operating room where technicians performed autopsies. Anyone who died violently or suspiciously got an autopsy. If an old person who was sick died at home, the funeral home would come there and pick them up.

If, however, a younger person, like the *Girl in the Chair* in my coming detective book, died, they might go to the ME's office for an autopsy.

The instructors told us we were *lucky* because there was a double homicide the previous night, and today was their autopsy. Perhaps one of the lessons of the visit was the relative nature of luck because these two were having a real bad day.

The examination room was a continuation of the hall of bodies separated only by a half-wall. Technicians wheeled bodies directly from the hall to the examination room.

The homicide victims, cut from neck to groin, lay face up on parallel tables, and by the time we arrived, all their internal organs were gone. The technicians called them *canoes*.

The object of this exercise was to shock us. I can't imagine any other reason to subject a group of young cadets to a procedure they would never be a part of. They didn't teach physics and ballistics at the pistol range; I can't imagine why they thought this would be helpful.

The two techs who were readying the bodies for the doctor's inspection were preparing to remove the brain from one of the victims. As the twenty-five of us gathered around the table, one of the techs took a scalpel and ran it around the base of the first man's skull.

Several sensitive individuals chose to move to the back of the group.

I and several of my more fun-loving cadre stayed right up front, so we didn't miss anything. The techs looked at each other and snickered, thinking they were about to shock us.

The one by the body reached under the scalp of the poor individual on the table and pulled it forward over his face, exposing the top of his skull.

Joe was right behind me.

He said, "Wow, you really pulled the wool over his eyes."

The techs both bugged as we enjoyed a laugh at Joe's quip. The techs took a quick look at each other, nodded, and one-handed the other a bone-cutting tool. This was a tool with a small saw blade on the end.

He ran this around the outside of the skull and pulled the top of his skull completely off, exposing his brain.

Tom said, "I think you took a little too much off the top."

The techs reacted physically to this, as we enjoyed another chuckle at their expense. Their plan wasn't going well. They expected us to cringe at the whole affair. They were about to experience *us*.

I guess they figured there was one more trick up their sleeves, and they exchanged another knowing glance as the one reached into the man's skull, removed his brain and plopped it into a large butcher's scale hanging close by. We all watched as the scale registered the brain's weight.

The tech looked in our direction to see our reaction.

I said, "That'll be two dollars and ninety-eight cents, please."

The tech shouted, "You people are nuts!"

He threw his gloves into the nearest trash can and walked off.

We thought we got the best of them until our instructor told us, "We have one more stop to make."

He took us to the separate room where they kept the bodies, which were too spoiled to keep in the open area. Bodies badly decomposed, burned in a fire or badly dismembered shared this special room.

He called it the *stink-room*.

We followed along, still enjoying our chuckles, when he stepped back and told the first cadet to open the door and go in. We stepped into this giant walk-in closet containing bodies in various, unrecognizable states of decay piled on tables and slabs protruding from the walls like submarine bunks.

The smell hit like a freight train. It got into every pore of your body in addition to your nose, sinus, eyes and mouth.

Most of us recoiled out the way we came seconds after the smell hit us. They got their revenge for our attitude in the autopsy.

They did it right before lunch. It took the rest of the day to get the smell out of our nose, eyes and mouth. Many skipped lunch and opted for the nearest store for large, pungent cigars to eliminate the smell.

I noted in the coming years, almost all the ME's techs munched the same potent cigars. I didn't have to ask why.

Chapter 27

The Never-Ending Academy

My lifelong friend David and my entire family attended my graduation from the academy. The graduation was for our class and the one following, which they combined with us to total 200.

To save time, one officer from each class represented their class on stage. They chose me to represent ours.

I reminded the chief to return my salute. My first AS moment as a police officer. Anyone else would have known to walk away and ignore the fact the chief wasn't following the script we rehearsed, but I insisted on the closure.

I wanted my salute.

We were excited, having spent the last four months in the academy, and were eagerly awaiting our assignments. By assignments, I mean to which of the twenty-three police districts we would go.

Instead, they ordered us back to the academy the following Monday. No one seemed to know why, so a few of us went out to celebrate and ponder.

That Monday, instead of cadets, 200 police officers returned to the academy wearing the regular uniform and loaded revolvers.

I couldn't help wondering, "What did I miss?"

We sat for two days in rows of those cold beige folding chairs, with loaded guns clanking against them, and jostled each other, watching training film after training film. When the staff exhausted those, they started running, wait for it, cartoons.

Someone somewhere was getting desperate.

By Tuesday afternoon, we were beyond restless.

Joe possessed a quarterdeck voice that cut through noise and penetrated a room-like sound surround. The *ants in his pants* were making him spin in his seat.

On the stage was the same lieutenant who originally welcomed us to the academy. He reminded me of *Fred Rogers* in a police uniform trying to keep order.

The noise level was getting so bad in the room I almost couldn't stand it. It was approaching the level normal people shut out, but since I couldn't do that and keep up with the input, it was approaching my threshold.

The lieutenant's effort to keep us quiet wasn't working. The class alternately heckled and ignored him.

As frustration took over, he tried to shout. Try to picture Fred Rogers shouting.

It's like a tin horn with a sock in it.

He picked up the stage microphone and said, "Ok, settle down." (the ultimate cliché)

I was alternately watching him and looking around the auditorium. I tuned in to Joe halfway across the room because I could see something was happening around him. I wanted to hear what it was.

The lieutenant decided on a new tactic. One of our girls wore a big band-aid on her forehead. Now you need to know she was one of those persons who were unable to put a pillowcase on a pillow.

The lieutenant knew anytime he addressed a cadet by name, it got everyone's attention. Everyone focused on the cadet and stopped talking. I don't get it, but it works.

He called out, "Donna."

Everyone froze, the room got quiet; we turned and looked at Donna.

He said, "Donna, what happened to your forehead?"

Joe belted out, "She scratched it on a zipper."

Bedlam returned.

The room erupted into laughter, foot stomping and general chaos. The rapidity of it all startled me so much I didn't laugh with the rest of the group.

It was bad now, and I could see other instructors peeking in at the back of the hall to see what was happening. They didn't want to come in and make the lieutenant look bad, but it was loud.

The lieutenant was still trying to gain control.

He spoke into the mike, "Alright, settle down now. Quiet, please." in his monotone voice.

Things started to run out of steam, and the lieutenant felt he was finally getting things under control. I could see in the body language of the other instructors they thought he was, too, so they stayed in the back.

I could finally hear myself think and was watching with split attention.

Donna didn't know who she wanted to hit first, the lieutenant or Joe.

Joe was sporting his Cheshire cat smile.

The lieutenant continued, "Seriously, Donna. What happened to your forehead?"

Joe replied, "The guy who stole her chin came back for her forehead."

The place erupted into greater chaos than before. I thought the lieutenant would faint. A howling laughter erupted from the NE boys[12] that sounded like the Rebel Yell.

Donna was slowly shaking her head.

The lieutenant froze with his mouth open.

Even I laughed this time.

In came the troops, Lieutenant Strong in the lead. Nobody messed with Lieutenant Strong.

---

[12] Philly is neighborhood oriented. I was from SW - very working-class type of area - more streetwise. The NE was the newer part of the city, had newer houses, schools and in general more money. The NE boys stuck closely together.

Chapter 28

Finally

"Alright, cut this shit out!" Strong shouted. He didn't need a microphone. He cast his eyes around the room and made eye contact with a few cadets. Silence slammed into the room as everyone instantly fell quiet.

Strong went to the front of the room, followed by an entourage of brass.

He held a clipboard with a list.

"Listen up," he said. "Anyone whose name is called, leave the auditorium and go to room 102."

He called about a dozen names. Their faces said they knew something. Each of them stood, looked around at us and left.

I didn't like the looks they gave us.

We wondered for a second what that was about, then realized our girls went with them. Something was up. Something that *wasn't-bad-for-them*.

"Alright." Strong continued when they were gone. "When you hear your name called, start filling in the front row from left to right."

He pointed at the left-most seat in the front row, as we saw it, and began to read names from the list. After reading forty or so names, he said, "Leave an empty row."

He called more names.

This went through four iterations. When he finished there were four groups of us with a row between each. I was in the second group.

He said, "You are the new four squads of the 17th District. You are now receiving a packet of information *about* the 17th District."

I found myself a member of the newly formed *two-squad,* watching instructors handing out overstuffed manila envelopes.

"Inside these envelopes," continued Strong, "Are maps of the 17th District showing sector boundaries and car numbers. Some things to note about the 17th District:"

- There are no hospitals in the 17th District,

- There is no place to eat on midnight to eight in the 17th District,

- When you arrive in the 17th District, there will be no veteran police officers,

- The academy staff will accompany you for a short period of time when you hit the street,

- Night command[13] will have a heavy presence in the district in the coming weeks,

- The district is under surveillance by outside agencies, avoid contact (Non-Philly law enforcement),

- There is also a list of places that are *off limits,* including, and especially, the Broad Street Diner on the East side of the 1200 block of South Broad Street. Do *not* go in there,

- There is limited parking around the 17th District; arrive early so you can find somewhere to park.

[13] Uniformed internal affairs supervisors.

"Those of you who are in *two-squad*, go home now and get some sleep. You are first in. You are due on duty at midnight tonight. Report to 20th and Federal with all your gear. Good luck."

He didn't have to tell me twice. We knocked half of the chairs over as *two-squad* hit the street. At 2:10 PM, the academy was in my rear-view mirror.

I drove not home but straight to the 17th. I wanted to make sure I knew where it was so I was not late to work at midnight. I wasn't familiar with this part of South Philly, so I consulted my street guide. With GPS still in the future, we carried pocket guides to the matrix of streets that is Philly.

The district was not what I expected. It was small and packed into a crowded block of row houses attached to a firehouse. A small parking lot held police cars with no place to park for private cars.

I circled the block a couple of times.

It was, to me, strange; it *felt* strange.

The district headquarters was on a pie-shaped island formed by the intersection of 20th Street, Federal Street and Point Breeze Avenue, situated like the Flatiron Building in NYC, on a smaller scale.

I looked around at the people, and there were a lot of them. There was a bar on the corner with the doors open, and it was full. There was a state liquor store[14] about a block away with a line out in front.

I found out later this was the second busiest state store in PA. I pondered the busiest.

I made a couple more laps around the block and headed down Reed Street toward Broad Street to get my bearings.

---

[14] Wine and liquor are sold legally only in PA state operated stores, locally called State Stores.

I took a breath and headed home. Yeah, I got a lot of sleep that day.

I thought little about the boys and girls sent to other districts. I don't know where they went. When I saw them again, we were men and women.

I do know they missed the adventure of a lifetime!

Chapter 29

The Experiment

"Organized crime in America takes in over forty billion dollars a year and spends little on office supplies."

– Woody Allen

While doing some fact-checking for the book, I heard from several of my 17th District Rookies that some critics labeled the experiment a failure. I would like to see the basis for that conclusion. Before *you* consider it, let me set the stage:

I read an article published in 2022 that details instances of corruption in the city dating as far back as 1907 and as late as 2020.

In 1971 The Pennsylvania Crime Commission officially opened an investigation after a series of articles in the Philadelphia Inquirer reported on misconduct in the 17th District.

The captain of the adjoining district resigned. A local newspaper interviewed him. The article read, *"About 90 percent of the officers, I suppose, are well aware of the corruption in the department. I guess a little less than half actually participate in one way or another."*[15]

A former officer in the 17th said between 1967 and 1969, all but two officers in the whole district were corrupt. In 1971, with cases of corruption reported in 13 of 22 districts, the new commissioner, considered by many to be a *straight-arrow*, began a program of

[15] Philadelphia Daily News, Philadelphia, Pennsylvania • Fri, Jan 7, 1972 Page 3 https://www.newspapers.com/article/philadelphia-daily-news/55073495/ retrieved June 16, 2024

reassignments, moving seven police inspectors and 19 of 22 police captains.

The Pennsylvania Crime Commission released an 874-page report in 1974 in which they reported finding *"police corruption in Philadelphia is ongoing, widespread, systematic, and occurring at all levels..."*[16]

That Crime Commission investigation ended with the arrest of seven 17th District officers.

Public outcry was getting louder, including an appeal to Congress for an investigation focused on Philadelphia, citing a *"lack of confidence in police and the inability to determine which police are criminals and which ones aren't. We are quite aware many of the criminals which terrorize the community are men walking around with badges."*[17]

I remember other news stories during this period focused on one *South Philadelphia District.* I was in the academy when this was developing and was not privy to the planning about to affect the lives and careers of the two hundred of us.

In 1977, the 17th was again the focus of a corruption investigation, and the commissioner transferred 137 officers out of the district after the arrest of three officers for ignoring an illegal gambling operation.

The experiment began when they sent us, directly from the academy, to report the same day at midnight, literally and figuratively in the dark.

We heard rumors we were replacing corrupt cops but didn't understand the full depth and breadth of the situation. The illegal gambling was only one aspect. We heard stories of brutality we found hard to visualize.

---

[16] Report on police corruption and the quality of law enforcement in Philadelphia / the Pennsylvania Crime Commission.
by Pennsylvania Crime Commission. https://archive.org/details/reportonpoliceco00penn

[17] Cassell, James. "PUSH Wants Congress to Investigate Local Criminal Justice System." Philadelphia Tribune (1912-), Apr 23, 1974. https://www.proquest.com/historical-newspapers/push-wants-congress-investigate-local-criminal/docview/532635908/se-2.

In addition to the overall foul atmosphere of the place, the transferred officers left us with a citizenry primed and prepared to resist us as veritable occupiers.

A select few from our class went to other districts. They also excluded all the women, as my best guess is they considered the situation where we were going, too perilous for them.

They sent us into a place savaged by people whom the department characterized worthy of immediate expulsion, replacing them with kids with guns.

When we arrived, we found sabotaged keyless police cars, vandalized facilities and missing street signs. We also found gangs, drugs, guns and packs of feral dogs.

We came at midnight to an abandoned police station.

Those sent to *observe* – *observed* as we waded into crowds, responded to homicides, and fought with gangs.

The only time I can remember we fumbled a call was the *first night in,* which a full complement of these observers should have prevented. They were there for precisely that reason. When *we* broke it down afterwards, we found one of them *caused* the problem. I can remember none that occurred after they finally left.

In the time we were there, overall crime went down, including motor vehicle crime, resulting in the removal of most of the selective enforcement zones[18] from the district because of fewer auto accidents.

We captured murderers, burglars, robbers, thieves and drug dealers in unprecedented numbers. Surprising what you can accomplish when you *focus on police work.*

---

[18] High accident areas were labeled Selective Enforcement Zones. If one was on your sector you were expected to write traffic tickets for the violations that Traffic Engineers had identified as the cause for so many accidents.

When six inmates escaped from prison and hid in the 17th, thinking the dumb rookies wouldn't find them, we bagged and returned them within a few days.

I can recall no arrests of police officers among the four squads during *our* time there, putting a decisive end to the bi-yearly sweeps and arrests of police officers in the district despite outright stalking by outside agencies, on- and off-duty.

Prior to that, it was a virtual apple orchard for arrests of police officers.

The 2022 article I read cites no incidents of arrests of police officers from the 17th *after* our arrival.

In 1983, however, they were able to catch the boss in charge of the whole mess in a sweep related to conspiracy, bribery, the extortion of money and other considerations to protect prostitution and vice activities.

Five indictments came from that sweep. They labeled him an *unindicted co-conspirator*, but this was years after he left the 17th. He was involved in the type of behavior, with the kind of people they sent him to eliminate.

And, he was not *one of us* in the strictest sense. He was around a lot longer than us and was supposed to be the role model.

Sounds systemic vs. a failure on our part.

If it *was* a failure, it wasn't on us.

Anyone from the three classes sent there boasts of their service in the 17th and proudly wears the forever badge as one of *The Rookies*.

I experienced more fun and excitement in my time in the 17th than at any time before or since.

Chapter 30

First In

If the 17th wasn't enough of a dump before we got there, it certainly was after the officers on nightwork got the news of their transfer. When the transfers came on the 11:00 PM teletype message, they dropped everything and left.

On their way out, they slashed tires on some police cars, pulled wires out under the hoods on others, and generally did everything but relieve themselves on the floor in the locker room. They emptied their lockers and threw anything they didn't want on the floor. You wouldn't believe how much crap people, especially cops, can accumulate in a locker.

Worn-out shoes, nasty parts of uniforms, broken gear of all sorts, moldy old Playboy and Hustler magazines, soda cans, candy wrappers, torn report books, dried-out pens, dead batteries, stanky sox, and other underwear.

There were papers of every sort: old hot sheets, mug shots, wanted posters and long tractor paper printouts from the computer listing the names of the transferees.

We arrived to find broken locker doors and toilet seats, missing light bulbs, holes in walls, and general disorder.

I thought this was bad until they returned later that night.

I left my gear in the trunk of my car to give the workers a chance to get the locker room in some kind of order. I arrived at eleven thirty that evening; it was chaos.

The place was full of brass, some of whom I recognized from the academy. Since the transferred officers left shortly after the notifications at eleven, there were no 17th District patrol cars on the streets for the past half hour.

There would be no one for at least another half hour.

From 11:00 PM until 12:20 AM, some academy personnel, the burglary team, the ACT[19] Teams, Highway Patrol[20] and some others responded to *some* calls. The regular officers, the ones who answered *all* calls from 911, were all gone.

I was lucky. I missed all the outgoing officers by fifteen minutes. When I arrived, there was only the corporal and one other officer in the operations room and guys I knew from the academy.

There were no women police officers. Those who were in my academy class went to districts where there were veteran officers to *ease* them into police work.

We were on our own.

---

[19] Plain-clothed "Anti-crime Teams" utilized in high crime areas.
[20] Internal unit of the Phila. Police Department who patrolled the two highways running through Philly and patrolled high crime areas in search of guns, drugs and felonies. They wore a distinctive variation of the regular uniform with crushed hats, riding boots and breaches. They worked the highways in marked cars and inner-city as "line-quad teams" utilizing motorcycles and unmarked cars.

Chapter 31

First Roll Call

I stood roll call the first night with 25 classmates fresh out of the academy in an atmosphere of unprecedented activity and excitement.

They still held two roll calls despite the fact we were all there at the same time. Normally, the two roll calls are a half-hour apart. We stood off to the side to watch the first group finish.

Sprinkled among our two graduating classes were a few officers who graduated in the class before us. They were angry. Originally sent to park districts in a holding pattern; they thought they were in their permanent assignments until notified to report to the 17th.

In the main, they were not happy campers.

With them, we were at a full complement of two hundred. The largest number of officers assigned to one district in a long while.

Unlike veteran officers who were in various stages of their careers, were sick, were on days off, were on vacation et cetera, we were brand new. With no sick days, no vacation and no holidays in the bank, we were *all* there.

The captain of the district was there. It was one of the few times I saw him in uniform.

There was a full complement of supervisors. A lieutenant and both sergeants. And there was an operations room crew, plus the academy personnel.

The captain gave a speech welcoming us to the district. This was one of the last times I saw him smile.

He introduced the supervisors and the *burglary team*, the plainclothes officers who worked in the district. He introduced them at each roll call, so we knew who they were and didn't shoot them.

Then came questions: In addition to the street, they needed people to work inside. Someone to keep track of the prisoners in the cell room and someone to work in the operations room with the corporal.

The corporal stepped up and asked, "Does anyone here know how to type?"

I learned to touch type when I was eight. There was no way I was working inside. I looked at my feet and tried to appear invisible.

Then he asked, "Has anyone here ever worked in a prison?" They needed a *turnkey*, an officer whose sole duty was to watch over prisoners in the cell room, a temporary holding place for people we arrested.

I was surprised he got immediate volunteers; to each his own.

Now came the good part. First, there was an inspection. The sergeant came by and looked at everyone's stuff. He was making sure we brought all our gear, that our uniforms were correct and that we remembered to put bullets in our guns.

Then he stood back and picked up a clipboard. He started to call out names.

Cubbage, 1712.

I got my own car on day one.

There are a lot of moving parts in a police district. A good example is all officers have their own keys to the police cars they use. This is so they never lose the key that comes from the operations room keyboard.

Even though all the cars use the same key, you still need one. Over the years, the board that used to hold one key for each car became bereft of keys because there was no reason to maintain it.

So, here we are, we all have our assignments, and some of us have no keys.

Luckily, there was one on the board for 1712, so I grabbed it and was gone.

The bosses woke a local locksmith to make extra keys so they could deploy all the cars.

The first chance I got, I got two duplicates made of the key, one to use and one as a spare.

That night was unbelievably full of stimulus. The idea of being alone on your own in a big city police car. The first night out. What a thrill, what a rush.

Most of us were in our early twenties. I was among the youngest at twenty-three. Although there were a couple who were so young, they needed special permission to buy an off-duty gun because the minimum age for owning a handgun in PA was twenty-one.

There were some who were in their thirties and a few at the maximum age of thirty-five. You might think they would have been a source of wisdom, being a little older, but....

Think about them just settling into adult life at thirty-five and leave it at that.

The first thing I did was make sure everything worked on my car. I checked the lights and siren (got to have your priorities), checked the tires and oil level, made sure there were no dents in it and drove off.

I checked the radio by calling for a radio check, the start of my love affair with Police Radio.

I drove straight to Washington Avenue, where I figured I could find the most traffic/trouble. I wasn't disappointed. Within a few minutes there was all sorts of disorder happening on that street. Cars with headlights out, cars with tail lights out, cars going through red lights, it was a veritable cornucopia of malfeasance. It also wasn't long before I was getting a call from Police Radio:

Dispatcher: *"1712"*

Me: *"1712"*

Dispatcher: *"CRD 2760"*

Me: *"1712 OK"*

CRD means Call Radio Dispatch at the extension given. The dispatcher answered the phone.

He said, "Who are you?"

I told him.

He said, "What are all these cars you're stopping?"

I said, "Well, one was missing taillight, the other a headlight...."

He cut me off, "Listen, kid. It's too busy for you to be tying up the radio for all these bullshit car-stops. Use a little discretion, will ya?"

"Ok," I said. "Sorry."

I don't know why I was sorry, but he seemed pissed off. I wondered who was going to catch all these cars, if I didn't do it.

I told him, "Ok, I'll be more selective."

He said, "That a boy." and hung up.

Remember the eidetic memory? Several times that night I remember hearing some confusing radio traffic concerning someone named Sammy Smith. There was a call coming in from an address that no one seemed to be able to find. This wasn't a surprise since many of the street signs were missing.

After several attempts by several patrol cars to find the place, a call came from one of the academy cars.

A lieutenant said, "Radio, that's obviously an unfounded call. Disregard any more calls from that address."

Radio acknowledged this and disregarded any more calls that night.

The night went so fast it was a blur. Zooming up and down Washington Avenue. Stopping cars, monitoring the radio, and answering calls, but I do remember clearly when the *Old 17th* showed up.

Chapter 32

The Old 17th

I was sitting on Washington Avenue, writing in my log, when I noticed a car coming in the opposite direction, driving erratically. Erratically like they were doing it on purpose, which they were.

It was about 4:00 AM. The car approached 20th Street, where the light was red; it slowed a little and then went right through the red.

I thought, "Can't they see the police car?"

I made a U-turn and went after them. I stopped them a half block later.

It was a large car. It stopped in the middle of the street, and three of the five occupants jumped out. I got a quick glimpse of shiny uniform shoes and a blue stripe down one guy's pants.

They were all clean cut, short hair, clean shaven and conservatively dressed. I realized I stopped a carload of drunken off-duty cops.

These were the guys, only hours earlier, displaced from the 17th. They were working night work when the transfers came out and immediately did what all good cops do when under pressure. They had gone on a bender.

They couldn't help themselves; they came back to mess with us. I was the lucky recipient of their mission. Before I could react (I naturally hesitated because they were police officers.), they were all over me.

Two of them bumped against me with their arms by their sides like high school kids on a basketball court.

A third pulled at the spotlight on my car, screaming, "Like to point this in my eyes, huh?"

I could understand they were upset about the transfers, but what did I have to do with that? I didn't want to get in a fight with them for two reasons: they were brother officers, or I thought so, and there were five of them.

I realized quickly I wasn't going to be able to control them physically, so I got an idea.

I started laughing.

I said, "Oh, I get it. You are the assholes we replaced. Thanks a lot for trashing the district for us; a nice way to break us in. Do you welcome all new cops this way? I guess we're lucky you're gone."

They froze. The two in the car came running out to hear what I was saying.

I continued, "We've heard all about you, so I guess you heard all the rumors about us too; we're spies, we're working for the feds, all that shit?"

"Well, don't let me disappoint you. Watch this."

As I was picking up the radio handset from inside the car, I continued to talk to them.

I said, "Let me see if I can remember this from the academy. OK, drunk off duty, 10-day suspension, drunk off duty in partial uniform, 20-day suspension, drunk off duty operating a motor vehicle, 30-day suspension."

"Oh, and My favorite, drunk off duty and arrested, 6 months suspension."

At this point, I keyed the radio and said, *"1712."*

The dispatcher responded, *"1712."*

I let go of the mike button, so I was no longer transmitting to the dispatcher; the cops didn't know this.

I said into the mike, *"1712, I'm in the 2000 block of Washington Avenue with a 1037 (DUI), five male occupants, unruly and belligerent; please send me a wagon and a supervisor."*

They thought I was broadcasting live to radio. You should have seen the looks on their faces. I could see one guy's hair stand up. Holy shit, they thought. These rookies *are* everything they said about them. They're crazy.

You've never seen five drunks get into a car so fast in your life. These clowns literally dove back into that glass house and were spinning wheels to get out of there before three of the four doors shut.

I can still see the bug eyes of one guy through the rear window of the car as they sped away. Hah.

"1712…," came the voice from my radio. *"1712, what's your message?"*

"Disregard, radio," I said.

"Ok, 1712" came the response.

Yeah, and *I'm* the "rookie".

Two more days of midnights, long roll calls, and more instructions. Here's what you did wrong last night: Blah, blah, blah.

In the early days, four or five cars would show up each time I made a car stop. Some with academy markings, some marked night command and some with no markings at all. *Markings* is cop talk for the identifying numbers and letters on patrol cars and wagons, indicating what district or unit they represent. Hence, the terms: *marked* and *unmarked* cars.

The unmarked Chrysler products didn't bother me; that was either Internal Affairs (IA) or Highway Patrol.

It was the unmarked Ford products I didn't like. Always the same: two males, thirties, suits, not sport coats, white shirts and always far enough away you couldn't get a good look. These were the outside agencies.

I sometimes spotted them following me, and was also starting to hear stories about them following some of us home after work.

I chalked it up to paranoia until my turn came.

I thought a lot about that time. There was a lot to process.

The new job, the excitement, amid all that, something stands out.

When the shit hit the fan, whenever there was any danger or potential for trouble, the only people who got out of any of those cars were the real cops.

None of the academy staff, no one from IA or night command, and especially not the outside agencies.

No, when the shit happened, it was my fellow rookies, the ACT teams, and you could always count on Highway Patrol to wade into anything to help you in a pinch.

Since I knew some officers in Highway, there was always someone from that unit shadowing me in those first weeks. I met a lot of line squad men like Jimmy and others tasked to "Keep an eye on the kid."

Jimmy watched my back and pulled me out of more than a couple of tight spots.

Chapter 33

A Guardian Angel

Jimmy was the epitome of what Highway Patrol was meant to be. He was tall, slim and took no crap from anyone. He was, however, fair and sensible. Unlike the stereotype of Highway, *over-reactive*, something to prove, and always over the edge, Jimmy was calm and professional.

But, if the SHTF, he was the one to have with you.

I first saw him at about 2:00 AM during a car stop. He showed to back me up in an unmarked car. I assumed he was stopping to watch my back, like any cop would do. He arrived from the oncoming direction, so the driver of the car I stopped could see the unmarked car. Jimmy watched from his car, and when I finished with the car stop, I looked over and waved thanks.

In this instance, the driver of the car I stopped knew the significance of the unmarked car. He knew there was a Highway Officer in there.

Jimmy waved and left.

One night, I was about to do something stupid, like smack someone, who lipped off to me when he stepped out of shadow and said, "Let's talk about what you're about to do."

I saw Jimmy often. He always gave me enough rope to do my own thing but was close enough to step in or pull me back if necessary.

Often, it was enough for him to step out of his car.

The sight of Highway Patrol in their crushed caps, breeches and boots often took the steam out of unruly people, the people who called them *Boot Cops*.

Chapter 34

The Robber in the Projects

The first time someone shoots at you, it's a little unnerving.

I'm sure everyone knows the term firing pin associated with guns. The terms most folks are unfamiliar with include cylinder, timing, primer, ratchet and pawl.

You don't need to know what all that means any more than you need to understand the inner workings of an antique watch, but you do need to know, like the watch, everything needs to be in time, or nothing works right.

If the primer, the thing the firing pin strikes to fire the bullet, is misaligned, and we're talking about being off by as little as $1/64^{th}$ of an inch, the gun might misfire. What you get is an off-center dent in the primer and no bang.

Nightwork follows midnights, it's when most of the activity happens. Dark is coming, so are monsters.

When midnights ended, I faced two days off before I could get back into the fray, making the world safe. And, it was a long two days, what we called *the big apple*.

If midnights ends on a Friday, you are off from eight in the morning Friday through Saturday and Sunday (your *RDOs* or *Regular Days Off*), and you don't have to be back to work until four in the afternoon Monday.

This is *the big apple*, almost a four-day weekend.

I was looking forward to nightwork because the academy and cop friends said everything happened on nightwork. They weren't kidding.

The bosses were still trying to figure out what to do with us, and I hadn't particularly messed up yet, so patrol car 1712 was still mine. The sergeant eventually reassigned me another car, and the guy who replaced me on 1712 rode it for 20 years.

I did my usual routine despite solid advice not to. I checked the oil, checked the lights, and checked the car for damage. I filled the gas tank in case I needed to pursue someone to the seashore.

The same rule applied to damage on the police car as applied to burglaries in your sector. If you were the first to find it, it was on the guy you relieved. If your relief found it, it was on you.

After I did my routine check, I went straight to Washington Avenue to see if I could get a ticket or two, or more, before things started to get busy. I stopped a couple of cars. Made some new friends and was about to make a run to the perimeter of my sector when the call came out.

In the 17th District. 1500 Point Breeze Avenue. On the highway. Robbery point of gun. Committed by a male, black leather jacket and blue jeans. Last seen on foot southbound on Point Breeze in the 1500 block.

Now, my route to work passed by this area of the district, and I remembered seeing a low-rise project in this block.

My neighbor, a veteran police officer, told me, "When a robbery call comes out, if you're not the car assigned, don't go to the scene. Figure out where the bad guy is going and go there and wait for him."

I considered three possibilities:

1. Across the 25th Street demarcation zone toward the West side of the district,

2. Into the 1st District to confuse the cops,

3. The project.

I chose the project.

Along with the academy staff, and other observers, poachers were appearing on our calls. Burglary teams from other districts were among them. Our 17th District Burglary team was awesome. Some of the others, I was to find out today, not so much.

I rolled up to Point Breeze Avenue and pulled my car over to the left side of the street. As I opened the door and started to move toward the project, I saw two men in plain clothes moving toward the project.

I looked at them sideways but thought they carried guns, and how else would they know to be there if they weren't police officers?

One of them saw me. He looked like Alfred E. Neumann on a bad hair day. The other looked like a bad Fonzie impressionist.

The bad hair called over, "He ran in here."

They ran through the parking lot of the project right down the middle, which gave me the creeps. The way they ran, flanked on either side by low-rise buildings with large standing bushes, shouted danger. The intense overhead lights, the kind around all city installations, could give you a sunburn.

It was just getting dark, too. The worst time of day for visibility. I thought a little more caution was in order. So, I drew my revolver and started to move cautiously down the lane in the shadow of the bushes.

These bushes were overgrown and taller than me. And, close enough together, they touched.

I was creeping along, checking both sides in case our bad guy was taking cover in one of these bushes. You can say I was being over-cautious, and apparently, the burglary team thought so, too.

Bad hair called out, "Hey. What are you doing? Come over here!"

I froze. I looked at him standing under the light in the middle of a project parking lot. I thought of a police officer – shot the previous year – standing under just such a light in a neighboring project.

He shouted again, "Hey. Can't you hear me? Get over here. And put that gun away."

OK, I thought, he's a veteran, he must know something I don't. Against my better judgment, I holstered my revolver, snapped it in place and stepped into the light.

Then I heard it. A revolver clicking is a creepy sound. The good thing is, if you can hear it *clicking*, it's not going *bang*. I swung my head around.

Standing just to my left, between two bushes, stood a male with a black leather jacket and blue jeans. He pointed a gun at my face, furiously pulling the trigger!

Luckily for me, he was either too stupid to load it, or it was out of time and misfiring. Either way, I didn't wait to find out. I hit the ground, and rolled up with my revolver at the ready.

He broke cover and ran. I pursued. He cleared the parking lot and crossed Point Breeze Avenue, gaining distance from me with every stride. He turned on Tasker Street. I made the same turn, losing ground. My last view of him was disappearing around the corner a half block away. When I reached the corner, he was nowhere in sight.

I walked back to my car, out of breath and furious. I wanted to avoid any more contact with them. I opened the door to leave, but the team wanted to lecture me.

They were going to teach this rookie something. They were about to realize they weren't in Kansas anymore.

The Fonzie one said, "Where did you go?"

I glared at him.

Many of the great, unwashed confuse the look I give, calling it a *deer-in-the-headlight* stare. What they don't know is they are experiencing the *eye of the tiger*. I was trying to decide which one I was going to smack first.

The one with the bad hair shouted, "Hey, where did you go? What do you think you're doing? Didn't you hear me tell you to come over here?"

I said, "Who the fuck are you?!"

He bowed up, and so did the other one. He said, "We're the (other district) Burglary team."

I said, "Well, this is the 17th District."

He said, "What's that supposed to mean?"

They came closer to me. I felt like a spider when a fly gets close to the web.

I said, "Which word didn't you understand? This is the 17th District. The other district is on the other side of Broad Street."

They still didn't get it. They got closer still. I reached in and picked up my hat and stick. I put the hat on and the stick under my arm.

I got closer and said loudly, "What don't you get? Do you know what you two stupid mother fuckers just did? Did you not see that asshole try to shoot me from the bushes?"

They looked at each other and back at me.

Hair said, "What are you talking about?"

I said, "Listen, I'm only going to say this once, so pay attention. Get the fuck out of my face and get the fuck off my sector."

They got a real case of the ass with this and started to move toward me when I reached for the stick.

I said, "You want to rethink this?"

They froze.

I said, "I'm giving you a choice. Get the fuck out of here on my say so, or tell it to my sergeant."

They backed up. They could see I wasn't kidding. They looked at each other, walked backwards a few steps, and said, "We'll see about this."

I responded, "Go fuck yourself."

They walked away cursing. I got into my car and left.

Now, this was one of many *what-did-I-do-to-myself-now* moments in the PD.

I don't mean the encounter with the bad guy; I mean the interaction with the veterans. I felt lucky to have escaped with no bullet wounds, so I returned to my car and resolved never to listen to a veteran again unless I knew them or someone I trusted vouched for them.

I was prepared to move on and forget the whole thing among cops, but not these two. When I got back to my car, I resumed patrol, but it wasn't more than ten minutes before the dispatcher called. The dispatcher ordered me to headquarters.

I arrived to find them talking to my sergeant. He asked me to come inside to the roll call room.

The sergeant Said, "I hear you had a run-in with the burglary team here."

I said, "Yeah, did they tell you what they did?"

He said, "They told me you wouldn't listen to them and ran off from the project."

I said, "Oh, yeah. Is what happened?"

I started toward the one with the big mouth. The sergeant stepped between us and said. Let's talk. He pulled me toward the JAD room.

I told him what happened.

His eyes bugged.

He asked me if they saw the guy.

I said they never saw him, walked right past him in the bushes, led me in front of him and didn't see when he tried to shoot me. They didn't even see him when he ran off, and I chased him a block and a half, trying to catch him. I told him the sonofabitch was too fast, and I lost him.

His eyes were as big as saucers.

He said, "What did you say to them?"

I told him I was going to leave until they started to fuck with me, and I told them to get the fuck off my sector. I also told them where *their* district was.

I added I told them they could either leave, because I told them, or I would bring him into it. I told him I thought they left.

He looked at me up and down.

He said, "He really tried to shoot you?"

I said, "Yeah, either he was empty, or his gun was a piece of shit, but he was working at it hard. I heard it cycle two or three times before I even saw him."

"I hit the ground and rolled up with my gun, but he was already running. I took off after him. I could hear the big-mouthed one yelling at me as I pursued the guy."

My Sergeant shook his head and said, "Ok, you *resume* (cop talk for *go back to work*). I'll take care of this."

I said, "OK." And left.

Five minutes later, I heard a radio call from my sergeant asking to meet with the lieutenant, a call from our lieutenant to the other district's lieutenant, and a call from their lieutenant to the burglary team.

111

The rumor was that all non-17th District persons got the order to stay out of the 17th District unless specifically ordered in. This included uniformed and plain clothes units. The plainclothes units got the additional order to present themselves to every 17th District roll call so each of the squads knew what they looked like in case they came in.

Other than that, their orders were, "Stay out!"

After that, the only units I saw were line squads with their partners, Stake-Out[21] in marked vehicles, and Jimmy by himself when he was in the neighborhood. It was always good to see him.

The others, rarely.

[21] Stake-Out was the original SWAT. They had a unit assigned to each division.

Chapter 35

"Why Don't You Do It?"

There were still instances of outside units showing up on our turf, even after the warning. Emboldened after the expulsion edict, I preemptively chased them off if they annoyed me.

In one instance, I was standing watching some random event on the street, and a line squad officer nearby came up to me and barked the order, "Go over there and do such and such."

I looked him in the eye. When he made eye contact, I dragged his eyes to his shirt sleeve, which was as slick as mine, no stripes. His eyes followed mine. I took the crease between my thumb and index finger like a soiled tissue.

I said, "When you get some stripes on these sleeves, come back and tell *me* what to do. In the interim, here's a thought: why don't *you* do it?"

He swelled to a point short of bursting.

We were standing side by side when this started, but he became incensed that I was challenging his authority, whatever he thought that was.

I thought, no, I knew we were the same rank, so he held no authority over me.

In his world, he was a veteran police officer, so all rookies must do his bidding.

In my world, there *were* no rookies.

He said, "Kid, who do you think you are? You're just a *rookie*."

I said, "First of all, I'm not your kid, and secondly, this is the 17th; there are *no rookies* here."

He squared up to me, but lacking the mirror neurons to tell me to do likewise, I kept my side to him. He didn't know what to do with this response or lack of response, so he continued to inflate, and I continued to ignore him.

With him sending me non-verbal messages I couldn't decipher and my flat affect sending back nothing in return, it was now a war of words. This is a bad move when your opponent has Aspergers.

I saw his eyes shift focus. The other *rookies* caught wind of what was happening, and now there was a crowd of five or six shoulder-surfing me looking at him.

I could feel them behind me. We were forming a habit of working so closely together we often maintained physical contact.

I don't know what he was thinking, but his eyes betrayed severe second thoughts.

He was having a life-changing experience. He was, for the first time in his life, on the wrong side of a group of unfriendly cops. Now challenged by a larger and unpredictable aggression, he rethought himself.

I was monitoring his partner standing nearby, as a partner should, watching his back. *He* eyed the group at *my* back.

He reached under his partner's arm and gave it a light tug.

His partner snapped out of his PTSD-infused state of confusion and looked at him. Their eyes met for a moment and the wireless communication beamed from his partner was, "Let's go."

He took one last look at me and my backup. He took a step back and left.

We could have a field day of analysis of this situation, but the message he took away was *when everyone is a rookie, no one is a rookie.* He suddenly found himself in a place he did not understand, so his best strategy was to retreat.

Things in the 17th District would continue to get curiouser and curiouser.

Chapter 36

Mutilated Driver's License

As a uniform street cop, especially during the first year, a lot of things hit me sideways. Things were especially foreign to me as an Aspie. This encounter compounded the issue.

I was on patrol when this scene unfolded: A large sedan approached, belching a cloud of blue smoke. The car was sliding through the stop signs, and when the driver *did* press the brake pedal, I could see one of the brake lights was out.

The car carried ten people. Although equipped with seats and belts for six people, I could see more than that from a quick glance.

After the driver coasted through the third stop sign in this densely populated area, I stopped him. I greeted him and looked in the car. There were nine young boys in the car. I asked for his driver's license and registration, eyeing the interior.

He handed me the registration and his license. I requested his date of birth because the top portion of the license was unreadable. At this time, licenses were still paper, and if you didn't get them laminated, the top would stick out of your wallet and get torn off, along with the driver's license number and date of birth.

I turned my attention to the boys. I could see they were comfortable in the car, indicating they knew the driver and were not under duress.

I asked one how he was doing and he replied in cheerful terms he was good. I asked him where he was going, and he said they were on the way to his aunt's house for dinner.

I asked the driver about all these boys in the car, and he said he was helping with folks who worked. He said that his sister took care of these boys during the day. This was not uncommon at this time, people running informal daycare centers.

I asked him why he wasn't stopping at the stop signs. He said the car would stall if he came to a complete stop, so he was coasting through them.

I went back to my car and called the radio dispatcher with the man's name and date of birth because I needed the driver's license number. The dispatcher told me he possessed a valid driver's license, providing the number.

He was also the registered owner. I mention this because it was rare to find anyone in this neighborhood with a license and fewer with registered cars.

I could have issued him several tickets. One for reckless driving for going through the three stop signs, one for the bad brake light, one for the bad exhaust system and several more for too many people in a car.

This would have amounted to over $350 worth of tickets, about *$1,700* in today's money.

Instead, I issued him one ticket. I issued him a ticket for a *mutilated license*. This is a non-moving violation which saved him from getting any points on his license. I told him I could have issued tickets for the stop signs, which were moving violations, and listed all the other ones I could have given him.

I told him if he went to the motor vehicle place and paid them fifty cents, they would give him a new license. If he took it to the traffic court across the street and showed them, they would dismiss the five-dollar ticket.

He gave me the worst stink-eye. He was angry. I asked him if he understood how many tickets I could have given him, and he said yes.

117

He and I were not on the same page. I asked him what the problem was.

He said, "My license ain't mutilated."

I said, "Sir, your license is *so* badly mutilated I couldn't read it. I had to call over the police radio to get the license number."

He said, "Well, if you could read it, you'd see *it don't mutilate 'til June.*"

I said, "Tell that to the judge."

He said, "I will." And drove off in a cloud of smoke.

I told this story to everyone who would listen. I found this to be incredibly funny.

About six months later, I was watching a popular T.V. cop show. In this episode, they acted out the exact story I just told you.

What are the chances that was a coincidence?

Chapter 37

Great Big German Shepherds

"Diplomacy is the art of saying 'Nice doggie' until you can find a rock."

— Will Rogers

An experience within the first few months on the street helped solidify my reliance on precise information. An experience that gave new meaning to the expression "Almost shit myself."

I was walking a footbeat.

That means my supervisor ordered me to a certain area and patrol from one point to another within a defined parameter boundary. Simply put, don't leave the 1200 block of Point Breeze Avenue, the street beside the police station.

This was the stick part of the carrots and sticks. I forget what I did; convenient, huh? But I was travelling on what the locals called *"The Shoe Leather Express"* for a day.

As I was walking to the spot, a woman screamed. It came from around the corner on Federal Street. As I rounded the corner, this scene unfolded:

Two well-built 60-pound German Shepherd dogs were backing a young woman into a corner created by the stairway to a row house and the front wall of that house. She was holding an infant in her arms, the dogs were snarling and baring their teeth.

She was terrified.

I wasn't sure what to do. My mind was full of things I *could* do. I wasn't sure what the law *allowed* me to do. My duty was to get the dogs off her, but I wasn't sure about my authority in the way I accomplished it.

I approached the dogs from behind. The woman was facing me.

I kicked the nearest dog in the nads. He yelped and backed off the woman, but the other one turned on me. It was winter, and I was clad in a leather jacket and wore military gloves consisting of a wool glove covered by a leather over-glove.

The dog grabbed my left hand, but the glove insulated my hand from his teeth while I pondered my next move.

The woman was able to slip away.

Here's the onion. One hand was in the dog's mouth, and the other on my service revolver. My initial thought was to simply shoot him. But I didn't know if I might do that.

Was I *allowed* to shoot a dog? What were the rules and rationale behind shooting a dog?

May you shoot the dog just because it's a dog?

I knew what dogs can do to people, and I was pretty sure the description of mayhem taught in the Crimes Code class in our training covered this, but it was a dog. I couldn't recall any mention of handling situations with dogs in the training.

While I was contemplating this, the other dog nursed his tender parts.

Einstein said, "Time is relative; its only worth depends upon what we do as it is passing."

It was passing fast!

I'm looking at my hand, monitoring the dog's progress as he tries to penetrate the leather; I'm keeping an eye on the other one who is licking his, well, you know. And I'm gripping the gun.

What to do?

Suddenly, a sharp whistle pierced the chaos, and both dogs took off at a run. They ran around the corner and into a house. There was a man with his head out the second-floor window. He was apparently in the habit of letting the dogs out to do their business and was now calling them back.

I gave him *what-fer* and went immediately into police headquarters across the street. I told the corporal to hold me out for a *personal* (toilet break).

I went to the head, but not before stopping off at my locker for the Crimes Code. In the Crime Code, I found something called *The Dog Laws*. Yes, you read correctly, The Dog Laws. See, my instincts were good. I know something must explain this situation.

I can still remember, as I sat in the men's room, letting my body decompress and my brain process what just happened, I found this:

Any officer in a city of the 1st Class [Philadelphia or Pittsburg] who observes a stray dog on the highway [anywhere outside] and does not destroy it is guilty of malfeasance of office[22].

I never saw a law like that. It *compelled* the summary destruction of all stray dogs on the streets of Philadelphia. Simply put, I certainly *could* have shot the dog, and under the laws of the Commonwealth of PA, *should* have shot the dog.

Now, knowing this, would I have shot the dog? Probably not, but I certainly would have tapped him on the head with a blackjack.

Later in my stay in the 17th, two feral dogs attacked me in an alley. I had no choice but to shoot them. That story comes later.

---

[22] Malfeasance in office is a wrongful act committed by a public official or employee while performing their duties. It can include: Intentionally failing to perform a required duty, Making decisions that are not in the best interests of the public, et Al.

The lesson I learned from the dog encounter was: learn more about the laws I enforced.

I lacked the instincts of the other officers, like the *fight-or-flight* response. I stood and processed the dog situation instead of reacting to it.

The whole event took less than a minute and thanks to the dog owner, vanished as quickly as it started.

Without the instincts, I *needed* the manual.

I made it a point to sit and read the manual, front to back, on my next day off.

And then turned my attention to the Motor Vehicle Code for similar treatment and similar reasons.

Chapter 38

Go to Radio

So, I hit the street in November, and by December, I managed to piss the dispatchers off so much that they convinced the bosses to detail me to the police radio room for a few week's training to see what it was like on the other side. They wanted me to feel their pain and take the lessons I learned back to my squad.

It's an AS stereotype that we have trouble talking on the phone. That's under normal circumstances; keep reading.

At that time, the folks answering the 911 calls and the dispatchers speaking directly to the police cars sat at the same console. The dispatchers sat on one side of a short wall, and the folks answering the phones sat on the other.

There were twelve consoles. One for each of the ten divisions, a city-wide J-Band and a utility or H-Band.

When the 911 line rang, someone answered, recorded the information on a pre-printed index card, and handed it over a wall to the dispatchers. There was a cubby on the top of the wall where you could stick the card so the dispatcher could see it, kind of like the cook in a diner sees the server's checks.

If it was a non-emergency call, like a meet complainant or disorderly crowd, you would stick it in the slot. If, however, it was an emergency, a robbery or a shooting, for example, you would get the dispatcher's attention and hand it directly to them.

Notice I didn't write *routine call*. We, the police, did nothing as a matter of routine.

I started out handling 911 calls and then trained on the dispatcher's side. They wanted me to see the chaos, acquire some empathy for them and not jam up the airways with unnecessary chatter. I got it. They couldn't handle important and dangerous calls with the air constantly busy with everyday stuff.

It turned out to be a positive experience, and I made some good friends and contacts.

Answering 911 was something else. I would return to radio for an extended period later in my career, but the 911 calls I answered in the short time in 1977 were a good wake-up.

People call for all sorts of nonsense.

I got a call one night from a woman who said, "I just gots the *call waiting* on my phone, and I needs to know…"

I cut her off, "Ma'am, this is the 911 emergency number."

She cut *me* off, "Shut up and listen to me."

I said, "Go ahead."

She said, "I just gots the call waiting on my phone. I needs to know: when I hear the tone, do I push the tix-tax-toe button or the astronaut?" (Just in case you're out-of-synch: the # *or the* *)

My instinct was to reiterate the 911 chant, but I suddenly got some sense and replied, "Press the astronaut." (See. I'm learning.)

"Thank you." came the cheery reply.

People called for leaky pipes, abandoned cars, parenting advice, referrals to doctors, tenant disputes and other nonsense. Of course, I also got the calls for burglaries, robberies, shootings and other emergencies.

The most frequent call was for a *disturbance house*. In the movies, they call these domestic disturbances.

I didn't know what to expect when I started to answer the phones, but I think I did expect a *little* decorum. You know, like, "Hi, this is so-and-so, and I'm calling to report a disturbance."

People dispense with the niceties when they call the police. Most of the calls for domestics started off like this:

Me: "911 Officer Cubbage, how can I help you?"

Them: "Get this motha-fucka out my house."

Or

Me: "911 Officer Cubbage, how can I help you?"

Them: "Send the PO-LEESE." (Then some screaming while I tried to get the address.)

Here's a notable event. Each event that occurs in the city gets a DC number or District Complaint number. It has the year number the district and a consecutively assigned number.

78-17-1 is the first DC number, in 1978, in the 17ᵗʰ District.

Shortly before midnight on December 31ˢᵗ it got quiet on the phones. The other personnel begged off for a break, and I found myself alone at the 911 console. I leaned back in my chair and put my hands behind my head, and as the clock struck midnight, every line on the console lit up at once.

I answered 20 calls in the span of two minutes, and each one was the same. Point Breeze Avenue and Federal Street, 20th and Federal, 20ᵗʰ Street and Point Breeze Avenue, 1200 Point Breeze Avenue, all in the same location on that pie shaped corner where district headquarters sat.

A shooting in the bar.

The dispatcher dispatched cars to the location on the same corner where I met the German Shepherds. On the floor of the bar, they found dead the first homicide victim of 1978.

DC# 78-17-1.

Happy New Year., Welcome to the 17ᵗʰ District.

Chapter 39

The Earps

The Good News? I brought friends *with* me!

I met Herc (Ecole Talone) the first morning on the way to the academy. I was about two blocks from the academy, on Academy Road, on which no one walks, and saw a young man walking wearing a white shirt, plain black pants and black uniform shoes. I thought, what are the chances?

I stopped and asked, "Are you on the way to the police academy?"

He smiled and said, "Yes."

I said, "Hop in."

He introduced himself as Hercules.

I looked at him and said, "Really, Hercules?"

He said, "Yes, but call me Herc."

I had made my first academy friend!

In most classrooms, I sat near Lou. You'll remember the story about Lou testing his handcuffs.

Tom also sat close by and was the only other redhead in the class. Did I mention I'm a redhead?

Joe sat near Herc in the academy; Joe joined the group as well.

After a few weeks, in the 17th, we became friendly with Ed, who was originally *not a happy camper*. They yanked him out of what he thought

127

was his permanent assignment in the park and sent him to the 17th with us. He was in the class ahead of us at the academy.

We all worked together and began to socialize off duty, so someone in one of the more elite cliques dubbed us *The Earps*. Their idea was we were like Wyatt Earp and his brothers who were Wild West sheriffs and exhibited behavior they considered *cowboy*.

BTW: the locals referred to the 17th District as *Dodge City*.

We grew to be able to depend on each other for backup on-duty and friends off-duty. Until the big boss kicked me out of two squad, we were in each other's constant company.

Chapter 40

Nick's Roast Beef

Among the well-kept secrets in South Philly in the 1970s was Nick's. Nick's was known for great roast beef sandwiches.

After the last night of night work, when the earthier members of the squad headed off for some watering hole or other, the Earps went to Nick's for the best roast beef on the best hard rolls topped with the best freshly cut parmesan, washed down by the best root beer on tap, ever.

We would sit, eat, laugh, tell war stories, exchange advice and generally try to figure out the meaning of life from our small slice of it. Not just any life, the one that included calls to fights, fires, floods, shootings, beatings and everything else under the sun and moon.

We debriefed on the week's events, the actions of our peers, what we did and what the supervisors did as a result. We compared notes, photos of bad guys, and strategies for catching them. Always mindful of the rule: no cops get hurt.

Sometimes we would make plans for one or more of our RDOs, *Regular Days Off,* like a visit to the range, a favorite gun shop, perhaps a dinner and a trip to South Street, maybe even a midnight viewing of the *Rocky Horror Picture Show* at the *Theatre of the Living Arts (TLA),* where the audience could participate in the movie.

The fact that we tanked up on root beer and roast beef vs. other libations eliminated other problems and always found us up early the next day, ready to go.

We were innocent, perhaps for the last time during those days, the first year after the academy. A time when the Earps were together, watching each other's backs and keeping each other's propensity to step on his poncho to a minimum.

When the Earps inevitably dispersed to other assignments, the potential for problems crept in, trouble increased, and innocence ended for us.

I began to see the differentiation among the morals of people in general, police officers in particular, and learned some new terms. I saw the difference between *good cops* and *bad cops,* and I received a new label, *A Straight-Arrow.*

It didn't make anything easier. If anything, it got worse for a while.

But, with time, distance and a little luck, I began to find my own way.

Chapter 41

Sector Cars

I mentioned in the last chapter that patrol car 1712 was still mine. One of the things obviously missing from our environment in the 17th was experience. We were green in almost every sense of the word. True, we came as a group better educated than many before us, but experience also has value. I was getting mine, as most do, through mistakes.

You may have picked up by now sergeants used a system of carrots and sticks. Carrots in the form of permanent assignments and sticks in the form of random details and foot-beats.

Sergeants did an impossible job. They determined who could go out and do the job without creating more mayhem. Let me break that down (just a little): patrol car 1712 was vastly different than 1711 car.

I don't know what I thought the job was going to be like. I knew what I saw in movies and T.V. shows where it appeared that police officers just drove around looking for trouble.

The police department divided districts into sectors. Each one was assigned a patrol car. One could also say each patrol car assigned a sector. Either way, when assigned a car at roll call, officers must stay on their sector. It was *their* sector. They were responsible for anything that happened there.

When someone called 911 and needed the police, the dispatcher sent the *sector car*. An officer could only leave their sector for a valid reason. Valid reasons included: another sector car was already busy. In that case, the dispatcher would choose someone to leave their sector, go into the other sector, handle the job, and go back to their own.

Officers may go to headquarters to drop off reports or take a bathroom break, called a *personal.*

But, if the dispatcher didn't send the officer somewhere, or there was some legitimate reason to leave, they must stay on their sectors.

Officers not permanently assigned to their own patrol car found life random and frustrating. Permanent is a loose word. Sergeants can change assignments at any time,

Each sector held unique qualities, like a small city. Were there main streets or a river? Who lived there, residents or factory workers? Was there a hospital?

I could go on, but you get the idea.

Sergeants learned the personalities of the officers. The sector patrol car 1712 covered with its main arteries and little mayhem vs., 1711 with small streets and lots of mayhem.

The sergeants tried to match the officers good at handling mayhem with 1711 because they could quell the mayhem, and if good at that, they seek mayhem. When they can't find it, they'll create it.

You want officers on patrol car 1712 who can sit quietly in a place with minimal mayhem, smoke cigarettes, and only move when necessary. They are content in 1712 car, but 1711 car would send them into meltdown, causing mayhem.

Once the sergeants figure it out, they concentrate on maintaining everyone's calm. When someone goes high and to the right, upsetting the calm, they have several tools at their disposal to bring them back to reality.

They'll start with something small, like a foot-beat for the day. This snaps most back to reality.

If not, they escalate by sending them to the bus for the day. This is a sort of exile. Sergeants can extend their stay to suit the level of non-conformance.

If this doesn't do the trick, more drastic measures are sometimes necessary to teach the lesson.

My cop-neighbor was fond of saying, "It's good to learn from your mistakes; it's better to learn from someone else's."

There was an officer in the position of learning this lesson for himself. He brought me the lesson so I could learn from him.

Chapter 42

A Valuable Lesson

"It is always advisable to perceive clearly our ignorance."

– Charles Darwin

There were good assignments and bad assignments. Here's a bad one.

There were good assignments within a district, and there were good assignments *special units* in the greater department. Special units were things like Highway Patrol, Stake Out and Traffic.

Each of these units came with perks.

Those who liked action went to Highway Patrol.

Stake Out was an *elite* unit requiring an Expert shooting badge.

There was a special unit for controlling the traffic in the city. Big city traffic includes rush hour on highways and major streets, and special events like concerts or sporting events. The Traffic Unit keeps this traffic flowing.

Traffic's charm was two-fold: One was it was almost all daywork. The other was *special posts*. Special posts were static, occurred on a routine and required little or no supervision.

An example could be an assignment to be at a specific busy intersection from seven in the morning until nine-thirty every weekday. Then, nothing until one in the afternoon, when traffic slowed, your call. Working daylight hours with and weekends off was a nice gig.

Removal from a special unit was bad. You're not just pulled out of your assigned car to walk a beat for a while. It upends your life. You might end up on midnights in some lousy district.

Imagine what you must have done for banishment from Traffic, into of all places, the 17th District. The rabbit hole of the department.

You must find a blue hat because traffic wears only white hats. You must find a uniform shirt with no patches because special units have patches on their uniforms; regular street cops wore none.

And, depending on how long you've been in traffic, you might have to scrounge up a stick, blackjack and other equipment because traffic cops never have any of that on them.

One nightwork, a stranger showed up in our midst. A new officer appeared at roll call. He was obviously a veteran because he was in his forties. He arrived amid the sarcastic departmental phrase, "No Further Information."

As you can imagine, the rumor mill went into overtime. The only thing we knew: he came from Traffic. We didn't know if he was temporary or permanent. I didn't have the network to get any info, so I just went to work.

The sergeant assigned him to a wagon. He was the replacement for whoever was off.

He would show up for work and go directly from his car to roll call, so there was no interaction possible with him in the locker room. He was already there for three days, and no one was any the wiser.

And, apparently, the bosses weren't talking. Neither was he, although, on the surface, he appeared a pleasant person, he was quiet. He didn't appear angry or put out.

One evening at about six, some typical disturbance erupted, resulting in an *assist* call. When I arrived, there was a large brawl in the middle of an intersection, and officers were wading in and pulling people out, trying to quiet it down.

The crowd identified the troublemaker. One of the officers handcuffed him.

The crowd was mad because he smacked a woman, precipitating the incident. The first officers to arrive could see the anger of the crowd and, fearing they would turn on them, called the assist.

This was yet another of those *alcohol-fueled* disturbances quickly diffused by removing the troublemaker. Wound up as he was, he insisted on struggling with the wagon crew as they took him to the wagon. He alternately cursed the officers and the crowd and howled at the moon.

I was standing at the back of the wagon with one hand on the back door, holding it so the crew could put him in. Prisoners would often recoil when entry to the wagon was imminent. As he approached and he saw the open wagon, he pulled loose from the officers.

I rushed toward him to help restrain him; we were face to face.

I said, "Stop this and get in the wagon."

He turned, looked me in the face and *spat* on me.

Without thinking, I balled my fist and pulled my arm back to punch him in the face.

My arm wouldn't move. It was in the grip of the officer from Traffic. What alarmed me more was although his grip on me was like a vice, his voice was calm and soft.

He leaned into my ear and said, "What are you going to tell the judge tomorrow?"

I looked him in the eyes.

He added, "When you stand up in court in front of the judge and have to explain how this guy got a black eye in handcuffs, how will you justify that?"

I went limp. He could feel it and let me go. Then he laughed.

The thing was, what he said to me, given the breadth of his experience, went right through me. I could picture the whole thing, trying to explain why I hit someone with handcuffs. I carried the lesson from that day on, in the department as well as afterwards. He, like a few others, taught me an incredibly valuable life lesson.

He taught me something only a veteran officer could, and it highlighted not only what we lacked when sent here but what it exposed us to on our own as rookies.

We became friendly, and I naturally asked what he was doing there. He said he got one of the bosses mad at him, but he was only there for the week. He would be back in traffic at the end of night work.

I thanked him vigorously for what he did.

I spread the story to anyone who would listen, hoping it would prevent them from the same potentially dangerous situation. I hoped for a contagion.

I was having about as much of an effect as a petunia in an onion patch.

I don't know how many caught it, but I do know some who didn't. There were some who walked themselves into situations I may have if not for the lesson.

Whenever something happens, even to this day, I can hear that calm, quiet voice saying, "What are you going to tell the judge tomorrow?"

If I could bottle it, I would.

Chapter 43

Tom's Horse

My dad grew up in the part of South Philly where I patrolled. Horses were common in his time. He told lots of stories about them. None like this one.

I was back in the 17th. Time for someone else's stint in the police radio room. I was back in my car. The dispatcher hit the alert tone. This is a tone that comes over the police radio before an important broadcast. It's meant to get your attention.

All cars in South Division. Be on the lookout for Mounted 1-A. Last seen in the area of 23rd and Passyunk.

Involuntarily, I looked at the radio – like that would help me understand the call. But it made no sense. Veteran officers could read into calls, but without their knowledge, the call made no sense to us.

The sergeant knew, though.

He got on the air and said, *"Radio, is that horse separated from its rider?"*

He knew that a horse was loose by the way it was broadcast. The dispatcher wasn't going to say, *"Yo, a horse is loose."* because civilians and the news monitored the air, and that didn't sound good.

Within a minute, Tom came on the air saying, *"176, I got him; he's running down 25th Street."*

I heard it before I saw it, and it was weird.

25th Street is six lanes wide, with an elevated concrete train trestle running down its center. Anything under the trestle echoed and carried for blocks.

What I heard was the loud, steady clip-clopping of approaching hooves in iron shoes.

I did the AS pause and let it sink in, like the sound of the surf. I thought: *Dad heard this as a child living here.* I knew it was one of those things in life I would never hear again.

Tom didn't have the siren going, but the lights were on. He was following this tall police horse trotting south on 25th Street.

The horse's handler, the *mounted officer* who rides the horse, came on the air and said, *"Don't chase him; follow along and see where he goes. Other cars run interference at cross streets and stop traffic."*

Tom continued to follow the horse, which looped back to Passyunk into a shopping center parking lot. Still winter, tall piles of snow, pushed there by plows and front-end loaders, created natural corrals. Tom watched the horse trot into the center of a horseshoe-shaped mound.

Tom pulled his car in front of the entrance and told the dispatcher, *"I have him trapped in the parking lot at 25th and Passyunk.",* followed by, *"Holy Shit!"*

The dispatcher said, *"176, are you OK?"*

He said, *"Yeah, I trapped him into a corner between two walls of snow and he just jumped over the hood of my car to get out. He's on the way back up 25th Street."*

I could see him coming back with several cars surrounding him. As he was passing me, a car pulled up close to him, and the passenger door opened. Apparently, the mounted man caught a ride with one of the 1st District cars and was now following his horse.

The car pulled next to the horse; the mounted man launched himself out of the car by putting his boots on the rocker panel. He vaulted through the air and caught the horn of the saddle.

The horse continued to run, dragging him as he tried to calm him. He was able to catch the dangling reins and finally brought the horse to a stop. I was amazed he was uninjured.

Another one of those stories you wouldn't believe if you hadn't seen it. A Wild West horse wrangling show on 25th Street in 1978.

What next?

Tom went on for days telling and retelling his story of the horse sailing over the hood of his car. It was a war story for the books.

Chapter 44

Confuse Me?

"Some people are hard to understand due to the improper excruciation of their words."

— The Author

I love the study of language. I minored in German in college and have a working knowledge of Flemish, Dutch and Yiddish. I've also studied Swedish and Norwegian.

None are as rich in nuance, color, usage, grammar and fluidity of construction as the King's.

I entitled a previous chapter, *Great Big German Shepherds,* in honor of a British friend who loves our colorfully overadjectized American expressions.

Throughout my schooling, including my first year of college, every class was English class. When I attended the Philadelphia College of Pharmacy & Science, there were no multiple guess tests given; any misspelled or misused word used in an answer rendered the entire answer wrong.

Irish and English nuns taught me in grammar school, and home was English class as well.

Among the neighborhood children, we could indulge in the SW Philly dialect, on the playground or streets and driveways, *acrossed the street, wherever we were at,* but at home, it was: "Speak correctly or else." At this point, with 23 years of correct English pounded into me, I was fairly familiar with the rules.

Add pedantry, an Aspie staple.

I'm also tuned into patterns. Children learn language listening to the spoken word, not from books, as one learns a foreign language in school. The children identify patterns of sounds that become their speech. The pattern of language is a music of sorts, and sour notes or missed meter breaks the pattern.

Breaks in patterns are a physical thing for me. It jolts me. Entering the 17th District, with its diversity of cultures, was rich with jolts.

The mixture of un- or under-educated people, first-generation immigrants, different life experiences and what-all-else rendered a miasma of misuse, mispronunciation, misinterpretation and otherwise mishandled, misappropriated and mutilated language.

At first, it jarred me and took time to translate the verbiage, pleonasm, and sometimes almost indecipherable utterances of my complainants, but I came to enjoy it. I began to collect little vignettes and phrases with a particularly fun ring.

I developed a talent for *tuning-in* to a person's unique accent, vernacular and creative use of English. After two full sentences, I could understand what they were saying.

What they were saying didn't always make sense, but I understood the words. This became particularly useful in later years when I edited tech manuals written by non-English-speaking contractors.

This introduction to word usages and contexts with which I was unfamiliar activated new and fun areas of my brain.

It all started one evening in a bar....

Chapter 45

"I'm a beep-beep Lady."

The dispatcher broadcast: *fight in the bar at 29ᵗʰ and Tasker*, the West end of the district. When I crossed 25th Street, the demographics changed. Fights in this area were usually fistfights.

Philly is known for the drastic changes in culture encountered by crossing a street. One area can be wholly Polish, the next street over Irish. Five blocks into the Irish neighborhood, it might become a Black or German neighborhood.

When I arrived, the sergeant was inside the bar. A wagon crew was busy quelling small scuffles, and other officers were arriving.

One particularly pickled individual grabbed his stool mate by the neck and punched him in the face.

The sergeant said, "Lock him up!"

The man swung around and said, "What for?"

The sergeant said, "You're *inebriated.*"

The man replied, "Don't call *me* dirty names."

The wagon crew grabbed him and started to handcuff him when I noticed another man reaching toward the sergeant's back. I grabbed him by the arm, and when I did, a hand came from behind and dug fingernails into my face.

I put my elbow into their ribs and swung around in a backhand, connecting with the jaw of a forty-year-old blond, launching her to the floor.

I pulled her up and was handcuffing her when she said, "Get your hands off me. I'm a *mother fucking lady*."

A jarringly new arrangement of slightly incongruous words.

My first instinct was to laugh, but the cuts on my face were beginning to throb, so it would have to wait.

Later that week I got a call for *a hospital case, a child*. I pulled out the stops, put the lights and siren on and went. It was on my side of 25th Street. When I arrived, there was a woman waiting with a little girl, and they got in the back seat.

Note: Trips to the hospital require the name of the sick person and the name of the doctor on the report.

On the way to the hospital, I asked, "Who is sick, you or the baby?"

She said, "She is. A bug crall in her ear and is tearin' her up."

I said, "Ok, what's her name?"

"Jones, jus like me." came the reply.

"What's her first name?" I asked.

"*Feemalay*," she replied.

"How do you spell that?" I asked.

"F-E-M-A-L-E," she replied.

I said, "That's *female*."

She snapped, "Don't look at me; the *hosipal* name her that."

It took a second or two for the image of the small beaded infant bracelet used in hospitals, reading, *Female Jones*, to display in my brain.

In the same year, I would meet another *Feemalay*. I also met a *Placenta* and a *Urine* pronounced *U-rine-ee*.

During a holiday gathering, I recounted this story, and my sister, who was a nurse in an inner-city maternity ward, said she also met a Urine. A woman was having a difficult pregnancy, and they needed to record her output. She hung a sign on a woman's bed to save her urine.

The sign read, "Save Urine."

When the baby was born, the mother named her Urine, explaining, "I appreciate the nurse who wrote that prayer for my baby while she was being born, so I kept the name."

My favorite remains, however, *Vagina*. Her mother pronounced it *Vageena*. An officer I was working with that day said to the mom, "You named your baby Vagina?"

The woman said, "Yes. I heard it in the hospital, and I liked it."

He looked at me, looked back at her and said, "That's a *pretty* name."

She smiled and said, "Thank you."

I took a woman to the hospital on another occasion. While helping her to the car, because she was limping badly, I asked what was wrong.

She said, "I got stuck in a *revolting* door, and it gave me *vertical* veins in my laigs. I needs the doctor to give me a *sub*scription."

I told the story to an officer from the NYPD.

He said, "The people in New York call varicose veins, *Syracuse* veins."

Anyone cut, shot, stabbed or otherwise *opened up*; cop talk for bleeding, got a *technical* shot. (tetanus)

One man hit another in the head with a *Mercedes*. (machete)

Met people who reported burglars crawling through their *transit*. (transom)

A man in court one day said he could see what happened so well at night because new lights had just been *erectified* on his street. (I'm sure you can figure that one out.)

The judge called a quick recess, ran into the adjoining hall and howled laughing.

And, I once comforted a crying five-year-old little girl because a neighborhood boy called her *pickle-head.*

Comparisons with what I learned would be odorous; it would be much ado to examination these good folks and true against my background and bless their tediousness with my pen and set down my excommunication against their everlasting redemption for their unjust usages and shall not write these plaintiffs down in white and black or ever call them ass.

"God save the foundation."

- Dogberry in Much Ado About Nothing by William Shakespeare

Chapter 46

Raspberry

Her name was as spicy as her personality.

In most districts, when an officer makes a pinch, they go directly to the detectives. We, however, were subject to having all *our* arrests screened before presenting them to the detectives. The screenings took place in the JAD room.

There was always something going on in there while we were new, so you could often poke your head in to see what was up. This day, some activity attracted my attention.

Two of my classmates were in there with two twenty-something women and a man of the same age. The man looked a bit inebriated and was leaning weakly against the desk. The two women were un-handcuffed as I walked in and became animated and vocal.

The story went: the man, a sailor from the local navy base, called the police and reported that the two women robbed him. He said they were prostitutes, and they took his money.

This is known as a *Murphy Game.* Usually, prostitutes get an inebriated man into a room where their pimp was waiting, and the pimp robbed them. *This* team acted independently and took this guy to a room and rolled him themselves.

The more vocal of the two women was Amerasian named Razzy, short for Raspberry. She was twenty-one years old. The other was white, nineteen and, by her own best guess, about eight months pregnant.

They both denied robbing the sailor.

Their version was he hired them both, but was too drunk to perform, so he felt he shouldn't have to pay.

They thought otherwise and either took his money or he paid and forgot. Either way, they were off to the detectives. They protested and continued to blame the man for the problem. They insisted he hired them and couldn't perform.

The women expected payment for services rendered. The fact that he failed on his end didn't cancel their contract.

Razzy shouted, "Look, he still has the rubber on."

One of the officers looked at me and laughed. He told the guy to pull down his pants. Sure enough, there was a condom hanging from his gear.

They packed everyone off for the detectives.

Later that day, the officer who made the pinch returned and told me, "That was Razzy's 100th arrest, making her the *most arrested* person in the city."

The detectives ran[25] her for a record and found 99 prior arrests for various crimes such as prostitution, obstructing the highway and disorderly conduct, crimes often used to arrest prostitutes.

This was her first felony arrest, she finally hit the big time.

---

[25] The act of entering a person's name into the National Crime Information Center or NCIC via computer was known as "running" them. When a person was taken into custody, the first thing a detective did was, "run them through the computer" to see if they were wanted on a warrant. Dispatchers also had access to NCIC to run people when an officer had a car stop. They could also determine if the person had a valid driver's license.

Chapter 47

Move

MOVE, a back-to-nature group, barricaded themselves in a house in West Philly. MOVE is not an acronym; it's supposed to mean they were always on the move or something equally fresh. Their profile rose when they pointed guns at their neighbors.

In a district properly staffed as ours, there were plenty of opportunities for *details* to other places because they needed the officers there more than in the 17th that day. One of these details was the MOVE detail. Remember, a detail is some assignment other than your regular one, like a parade or some other event.

The MOVE detail was a contingent of police officers surrounding the MOVE complex to keep them from terrorizing the neighborhood after numerous complaints that one of their members threatened the neighbors with a gun. Not just any gun, an AK-47 assault rifle.

The detail could last for days or weeks. This was the first time for me. I would be there for a week.

When I arrived, a detective approached.

He said, "Are you Cubbage?"

I said, "Yes".

I love one-word answers.

He said, "Is it true you know about guns?"

Now, understand in Philly in the 1970s, "Is it true you know about guns?" roughly translates to "Are you the gun expert?" Sometimes affectionately known as the "Gun Nut".

"Yes," I said again.

He said, "Come with me".

He led me to the staging area, a block or so from the compound, where there was a klatch of others in plain clothes.

The one who was obviously in charge looked up and said, "Is this him?"

The detective nodded.

The boss, a detective lieutenant, said, "I understand you know a lot about guns."

I upped my game to "Yes, sir."

He said, "Good, come with me".

We walked down the street directly toward the action, to a spot directly beside the complex. The complex was on a corner. We were on the side street, facing the side of the MOVE complex. A flat-sided brick building sidled up to the sidewalk on our side.

I could put my back against the side of this building and be facing the side of the platform in front of the MOVE house. From this vantage point, the danger that was readily apparent was the male standing on the parapet with an automatic rifle at port rest.

The lieutenant asked, "See the guy on the barricade?"

"The one with the AK-47?" I asked.

He laughed and said, "You're my man."

"Here's what I want you to do," he said as he handed me a hand-held radio.

"Keep an eye on the barricade. If anything changes, he does something different, or someone else comes out, call over radio and let them know."

I said, "OK, I can do that."

He said, "We asked for you because we need to know what kind of weapons they have, and we heard you're good with that."

I said I was.

Before he left, he looked me in the eye and said, "Whatever you do, don't shoot anyone."

I said, "What if he *points* that at me?"

"We got you covered."

"Why don't I feel good about that?"

He said, "Look across the street. See the windows on the second floor?" The front of the MOVE house faced this house.

I nodded.

He said, "There are three snipers and a .50 caliber machine gun behind those screens".

"Really?" I said?

He winked and nodded.

I said, "Ok".

He smiled, turned, and left.

For the next four hours I stood in the doorway and exchanged glances with my man with the AK-47. I got a break for lunch at noon and returned for the balance of the day.

The AK-man gritted on me, gave me the hairy eyeball and, on occasion, petted the AK. He ventured a slight turn in *my* direction on a couple of occasions, and I leaned toward *him*.

I think the game I was playing and his knowledge there was something bad behind those windows across the street kept him honest.

He didn't complete the turn and kept his muzzle pointed up, so I kept cool, watched him, and radioed in information.

I finished out the week in this way and went back to the 17th. Until my name came again a few months later.

Chapter 48

Move 2.0

I was at MOVE again and about to do something very Aspie. That is purposely precipitate a face-to-face encounter with The Chief, something most officers went *way* out of their way to avoid.

I reported that morning to a brand-new sergeant. I could tell this by his uniform. Detectives don't have to maintain a uniform, and many don't. Sudden promotion to sergeant prompts a trip to the uniform store. I knew this sergeant was a newly promoted detective. His gear was so new I could smell it.

Our favorite Chief Inspector oversaw the MOVE detail. Police Officers thought of him as a PITA, always a stickler for regulations, especially when it came to the uniform.

A frequent story was that he would see someone with a Sam Browne belt who did not take the time to polish the holes where the belt buckle fastened.

We got our uniform stuff from the lowest bidder, so when they punched the holes in the belt, they didn't bother to put any polish in there, so the holes were bare leather.

When the belt was new, you could see these holes from across the street.

Our sergeant was familiar with the uniform regulations, because he had just bought a new one. And as a supervisor, he now enforces those regulations.

I can attest to one AS characterization being accurate. Many of us dislike any article of clothing that sticks out and rubs against us, like the labels on a shirt or a lump from a tucked-in shirt.

Large silver buckles secured the garrison belt, the one that holds up your pants, and the Sam Browne belt, the one that carries your gun and other gear. There was a large buckle pushing against another large buckle. It was super uncomfortable.

It's a constant irritation and distraction. Neither is good when your attention should be on police work.

The first chance I got, I upgraded my rig to the latest and greatest. I replaced everything with new leather gear from a Western, read that cowboy-West outfitter.

My new belt was double-stitched and was twice as thick as the regular belt. The holster was the thumb break variety, which laid against your body with a slight cant, presenting the gun grips for a quicker draw.

This is much like the gear all U.S. police officers carry today. High up on the belt vs. the old hanging swivel holsters we were issued.

The most visible difference was that there was no visible metal. No buckles, neither the garrison belt nor the Sam Browne belt. Invisible hook-and-loop fabric secured the belts.

Very space-age looking.

As we got ready to start our day at the MOVE detail, the first order of business was a roll call with your supervisor. In my case, the new sergeant.

ASIDE: When we came out of the academy in 1977 and replaced the entire complement of the 17th District, there were all sorts of rumors floating around about us. One was we were all spies from the academy. Another was we were all undercover, working for the outside agencies. Yet another painted us as all liberal read that gay, college-educated lackeys of some governmental organization that infiltrated the PD for no good purpose. Still another reported we were all brainwashed, sticklers for the rules and were blindly loyal to upper management, the brass.

None of this sat well with veteran officers.

As we presented ourselves to the sergeant, we were directly across the street from a formation of bosses. All these guys wore white shirts and clustered together whenever the opportunity presented itself. This was *the brass*. They were all men. The first woman I saw in a white shirt or in any supervisory position was still in my future.

They were presently involved in their characteristic fawning ritual over the Chief. The Monty Pythons parody this behavior beautifully in the hospital scene in *The Meaning of Life*.

While this carnival atmosphere unfolded in front of me, the new sergeant was busy doing his duty: counting his men, making sure his list matched names, and generally being a noodge. It must be mandatory because there is always a speech somewhere in this roll call deal.

Remember the *Don't Shoot Anyone speech*? Well, this was the *Don't get me in trouble because I'm still on probation speech*. A new promotee is on probation for the first six months, subject to demotion to their previous rank, *a fate worse than death*.

The sergeant was giving us the lay of the land and summed it all up by saying, "And, be warned, that maniac chief inspector is here, so make sure your uniforms are all in order."

He said, "He's right over there." motioning across the street.

The chief was easy to recognize. I remembered him from field training, exaggeratedly good posture, pristine uniforms, elevator shoes – are they regulation?

As he's speaking, the sergeant is looking at everyone's belt. He's looking for the naked leathery belt holes the chief is famous for. As he gets to me, his eyes bug out of his head, and he shrieks, "Oh my God. Where is your belt buckle?"

"I don't have one." I calmly replied, making deliberate eye contact.

He starts to stutter, "Waaat? Oh, shit, don't let him see you. He's a madman." using the chief's nickname, *Mad-Man-Mike*.

We were all standing in a semi-circle in front of the sergeant; the other officers were beginning to move away from me toward the sergeant like I carried a contagious disease.

Normal people are so predictable.

Aspies aren't joiners. I looked from face to face and back to the sergeant.

Now, I don't like practical jokes, and I never set out on my own to concoct or play them, but when one as good as this falls in my lap, there was no choice.

After I caught the look of each of the men in the squad, I looked back at the sergeant.

I took a half step toward him and said, "Are you talking about the *chief inspectooor?*"

He froze. The other officers looked back and forth at us. I leaned a little forward.

I said, but with a softer and more feminine voice, "Are you making disparaging remarks about a *chief inspector* of the Philadelphia Police Department?"

I added a nice uplift to the word *department*. His eyes started to widen.

Then, I let them have the whole performance, shaking my head disapprovingly.

"Tisk, tisk, tisk", I made that girl noise with my tongue.

I shook my head in apparent disbelief and disapproval, a display of offense that someone would utter such a thing about a high-ranking member of the police department.

As expected, the other officers were beginning to show in their body language they felt like they made a mistake moving *toward* the sergeant.

Suddenly, *he* was the pariah.

The timing was perfect, I took another half-step forward to intensify the effect.

The others began to inch backward and watch me intently. The sergeant was frozen.

I said, adding a hint of lisp, "What do you think he would say if he heard what you said?"

A look of terror sprang onto the sergeant's face and one of disbelief onto the faces of all the others.

"I'm going to go tell him," I announced.

As I was turning on my heels to cross the street. The sergeant silently mouthed something, his feet firmly glued to the sidewalk. He reached for me with wilting arms.

I walked directly to the chief.

As I got close to the brass, they began to sense something. Something wasn't right. One by one, they stole glances with peripheral vision. As I got closer, they began to turn one by one despite the fact the chief was obviously telling an *all-engaging* story.

This was not something a cop, that's what I was, just a cop, would do, boldly walk up to the chief. They were all trying to figure out what was happening.

They couldn't.

The chief, with his right side at a 90-degree angle to my approach, gradually began to realize his audience's attention drifting away from his speech. At first, he looked for the answer among the faces before him but couldn't find it.

Then he realized they were looking to his right, so something must be happening over there.

He turned.

Just as he turned to face me, I reached the curb of the sidewalk where they were clustered. He saw me but couldn't process it.

Cops usually hid from him. Why was this one walking straight at him?

This wasn't making any sense to him any more than it was to the rest of the group.

As promised, he was staring directly at my belt, seeking those vexing, unpolished holes.

I was within touching distance of him. I stopped, came to attention, and presented arms, a perfect hand salute.

I stayed in the street, giving him an extra four inches of height. He was conscious of his height, hence the elevator shoes.

Gamesmanship.

After he stared at the place where the holes, not to mention the belt buckle, were *supposed to be* for what seemed like minutes, he finally looked up and realized he was supposed to return the salute.

He composed himself, snapped to attention and properly returned the salute.

I said, "Good Morning, chief."

He looked at my face, shifted his gaze to my name tag, made the connection and blurted out, "No shit. You related?"

"Yes, sir," I replied.

"What's your name?" he asked.

"Michael, sir. Just like yours," I snapped.

"No shit," he said again. He dropped his guard, came over, and threw his arm around my shoulder.

"You know," he said, "Saint Michael is the patron saint of police officers."

"Yes, sir I do. He's right here around my neck." I said as I patted my chest and the location of my Saint Michael medal.

"No shit," he said again.

Then he said, "What are you doing here?"

I told him I was from the 17th but detailed here for the week.

He said, "You know, I'm in charge of this whole detail."

"Wow," I said.

He smiled, waved his arm in the direction of the MOVE house and the men and equipment of the detail, and said he was "in charge" of the whole thing.

Then, with his arm still around my shoulders, he led me away, saying, "Let me show you around."

He took me on a 15-minute tour of the entire detail. Showed me the command post, where they staged the armored car and Trojan horses, pointing out that the Trojan horse[26] was his idea.

---

[26] Trojan horses were wagons stuffed with police officers - used during civil unrest to rush a bunch of police officers into the center of the action.

I told him it was a great idea. Worthy of Odysseus himself. I'm no fool. He replied with a proud smile.

By this time, we were back to the starting point. No one had moved because the day had not yet started. I had derailed it. The briefing was meant to kick off the day's activities, but now no one knew what to do until the chief got back and lit their fuses. The sergeant and the rest of my squad waited, frozen in place.

The chief said I should come and see him. I said I would.

At this point – to enhance the effect of the joke – I pointed directly at the sergeant.

I told the chief, "I was standing just over there, and thought it would be a good time to introduce myself."

Are you ready for this – there was a big tree on the sidewalk behind the sergeant. He ran and hid behind it! I couldn't believe it. This was great!

The chief looked at my belt again.

I said, "How do you like it? It takes a nice shine."

He said, "You know, I like it. I do."

I stepped back, came to attention, and presented arms.

The chief snapped to attention and returned the salute.

I said, "Thanks for the tour, chief. I'll come and see you."

"Do that," he replied.

"I like that belt," he called after me as I walked back to my group.

Now for the best part. I approached the squad, gave them a prissy look, sashayed through them and went straight to the sergeant's tree.

I stopped, put my hands on my hips and announced, "He wants to talk to you."

He deflated. His head slumped, his shoulders rounded, he got shorter, bent over and started to swoon.

He dragged first one foot and the other; as he was passing me, I said so everyone could hear it, "Hey, I'm just kidding. He's an old friend of my family, and they told me to introduce myself if I happened to see him."

My normal voice caught everyone by surprise.

He let out a huge sigh of relief.

The whole squad bellowed laughter.

"You're alright, kid." came the sentiment. "We thought…"

"Yeah, I know, the rookie from the 17th; I've heard the stories," I replied.

The laughter renewed itself as they slapped me on the back. The sergeant, who was now clearly relieved, even managed to smile a little.

I said, "Boss, if I ever take myself that seriously, someone needs to shoot me. Relax, and you'll be fine."

I put out my hand. He nodded in agreement, shook my hand and laughed.

"You had me going there for a while." he wheezed.

"I know," I said. "Sorry, but I couldn't resist."

He didn't know it, but my Mad-Man-Mike story was just as good.

Chapter 49

The Fine Art of Homicide

"Why does man kill? He kills for food. And not only food: frequently there must be a beverage."

— Woody Allen

I was back home in the 17th again. The call came out as a *shooting and a hospital case at the Cabaret on the 1800 block of Federal Street*. With a good slingshot, you could hit our district headquarters from there.

I zoomed over and found several cars already on location.

Apparently, there was a crowd of two hundred inside this club, which the folks called a *Cabaret*. The interior resembled those movie shots of Vegas clubs with a large bar on one side of an oval dance floor surrounded by multi-tiered seating.

As an Aspie, I'm always discovering patterns. The one I saw in almost all crimes I encountered was *alcohol*.

Sunny was one of the folks having fun at the cabaret. He noticed *Chaz* in the crowd. He and Chaz were in a long-running feud. Sunny came armed with a 9mm automatic pistol loaded with seven rounds of ammunition.

According to witnesses, Sunny wasted no time addressing his grievances with Chaz and simply drew the *nine* and started shooting. Chaz naturally reacted by *getting feet*.

Chaz ran around and among the two hundred patrons, ducking and dodging Sunny's fusillade. Witnesses said he jumped over the railing by the dance floor, through the scrambling dancers, vaulted the other railing, and ducked under tables trying to avoid the flying bullets and reach an exit.

Sonny, oblivious to the other partygoers, continued to track him and fire.

The 9mm round, designed for use in war, designed for penetration, is not a guided missile. Once Sunny launched it, he could not redirect it. It will often zip right through the first person and continue flight into one or more others.

As Sunny continued to try to reach out and touch Chaz, and Chaz continued to duck and dodge his attempts, the seven rounds of *his* nine found and penetrated nine people.

When Chaz finally hit the exit at the rear of the Cabaret and made good his escape unscathed, there were nine severely wounded people in the Cabaret, three of whom were stone-cold dead.

When Sunny came out in handcuffs, accompanied by two of my classmates, I was standing by the back of the wagon. The wagon crew took a moment to search him before putting him in.

Sunny turned to me and said, "I didn't mean to shoot any of those folks. I was shooting at Chaz. It doesn't count I hit the others, does it? It was an accident."

I said, "You know what? Tell that to the judge. The judge will understand."

He smiled and said, "Thank you."

The wagon crew shot me a smirk as they took him away.

Aspies are especially good at patterns, but I can't imagine why anyone hasn't identified this one. I'm thinking hard, trying to remember a shooting that *did not* involve alcohol.

Maybe we should consider it in the current gun debate.

Chapter 50

Four Assists - Some Kind of Record

I possess the *gift* of being able to make almost anyone angry; I can make some people insanely angry. I can consistently say the wrong thing and misinterpret what people say. I can drop turd after turd in the punchbowl and break anything social. The funny thing is, I can also talk the birds down out of the trees. I was in the process of doing just that when other officers showed up to *help*. This is why I can confidently say, "This particular shitstorm was not my fault."

I liked cars that bordered big streets, because I could run into other sectors if someone needed help fast. It was also an excuse to wander.

Patrol car 1711 was one of these cars.

My sergeant realized I could diffuse complicated situations in areas of chaos. He assigned me to 1711. He knew I was not good at sectors less busy because that's when I would get people angry.

1711 was a much better fit than 1712.

If there was chaos, I fixed it.

If there was no chaos, I rearranged things.

Normal people considered this a *form of chaos*.

In this instance, however, the dispatcher assigned me the incident. It was off my sector. I'm surprised; in hindsight, they sent only one car, but I guess the initial call didn't sound like something with the potential for trouble.

By the time it was over, it was a legend. A war story for the ages.

Two lines divided the district. 25th Street running north to south, and Washington Avenue running east to west.

On the East side of 25th Street, where my sector lay, were almost all Black folks.

The West side of 25th Street, called the West End, was mostly Irish.

The West End ran past 30th Street but began to change because the federal government built housing projects there, so the demographic changed a bit, but between 25th and 30th was solidly Irish.

On this lovely spring night, I got a call, *29th and Tasker, 2nd floor, loud party.*

What an understatement.

In a job full of surreal moments, this was a new one. When I pulled up on the scene, I could *feel* the music. I got out and looked at the building, the noise coming from it was so intense I swore the building was moving. It looked, sounded, and felt like it was jumping up and down.

My synesthesia[27] was kicking in. Maybe it was just me because of the condition, but that's how it felt.

As I got out of my car, I noticed a wagon crew, Bob and Len, also responded. They were there informally to watch my back.

The building in question was a two-story building on the corner. It was a club that would rent out for parties and such. The action was on the 2nd floor.

When I approached the door, there were a half-dozen teenagers on the top step in front of the door, and they pulled together to block my way into the club. The door was ajar.

---

[27] A condition where you experience one of your senses through another. Another AS "gift".

One got right up in my face and said, "You can't come in here."

I brushed him aside and went in.

When you entered this place, you were immediately confronted with a steep flight of stairs leading to the second floor. As soon as you stepped through the door, you were at the bottom of the stairs, heading straight up to the party. With walls on both sides, the staircase was a tunnel.

I walked to the top of the stairs, and I can't imagine I didn't have my mouth open with what I saw. I stood there for a moment, looking at over two hundred teenagers drunk off their asses.

The music was *soooo* loud I could feel it in my bones. The floor was undulating and the entire room was like a huge bussing, shouting, laughing hive. I stood for a moment, taking it in.

The only adult in the room, the bartender, was standing behind the bar to the left, frozen, looking at me. I told him to turn the music off.

My thought was to turn off the music, let the kids see me, and slowly start to slither out of the room. They would go somewhere else, but it resolved this problem.

He stood there frozen, and I went closer and shouted as loudly as I could, "Turn the music off!"

I asked him WTF, and he shrugged and said, "I just work here."

I was beginning a lecture when it happened.

Now, when the music went off, the kids didn't stop partying. They weren't dancing or anything, just enjoying the night. They continued what they were doing, enjoying the buzz left in their ears from the loud music and the buzz in their heads from the alcohol.

They hadn't noticed me yet. I was a few steps in from the top of the stairs.

Being at the top of the stairs was like being in the breech of a cannon. At one end were two hundred drunken teens, and at the other end of the tube, the street.

As I started my lecture to the bartender, one of the wagon crew, Bob, who was on the top step but not yet on the landing, leaned over the railing and shouted, "OK, everybody out!"

It came across loud and clear, filling the void left by the now-absent music.

At that, the kids all turned, got immediately frightened, panicked and ran for the stairwell.

Oh, did I mention there was no other way out? One way in and one way out. No other way out except second-story windows.

The stampede to the stairwell almost knocked me down the steps on my ass. I jumped to the side just in time.

Bob and Len ran just ahead of the flood of drunken teens pouring down the tunnel.

I thought, *"OK, this'll work."*

I went to the bartender to read him the riot act. His response would dictate whether he agreed to clean up and *lock up the club* for the night or I would lock *him* up for the night.

After about two or three minutes, as the kids were navigating the stairs trying to get out of the club, I heard a sound police officers immediately recognize and hate. The sound of a fist banging on the side of a police wagon.

I ran to the nearest window and looked out to see Bob and Len fighting with a crowd of about twenty angry eighteen-year-olds. The teen I had brushed by to enter the party was in handcuffs. Bob and Len were battling a crowd determined to free him.

I later learned this kid was the reason for the party. Apparently, he just graduated from the local high school. He saved up for years for this party and blew all his savings on the club and beer.

I shouted to the bartender, "Is there another way out?"

He said, "No, just those stairs."

I ran back to the window. The fight was getting worse. Many of the kids coming out of the club were joining in the fight.

I fought my way to the top of the stairs and shouted, "If you don't get out of my way, I'm going to climb down on top of your heads!"

That did the trick. In a matter of seconds, I cleared the steps and was back on the street.

I ran to my car and called an *Assist*.

I ran up behind the crowd surrounding the wagon crew and started pulling bodies off. There was a tug-of-war going on between the wagon crew and the crowd with the handcuffed teen.

I could hear the sirens of the approaching cars as I fought my way toward the wagon. I shoved several people off, and we made a path to the back of the wagon and locked the teen inside. Then, the real fight started.

The noise and the neighborhood grapevine activated the entire neighborhood. People were pouring into the streets from every house, rapidly swelling the two-hundred-plus crowd.

Instead of going home or finding some other place to party, all the boys stayed on to fight, and adults from the neighborhood joined in.

Most of the females were smart enough to go home because the crowd, at this point, was almost entirely male.

Someone punched me in the side of the head, and I swung my stick in his direction. I missed and he ran down Tasker Street with me in pursuit.

When I got a half-block away, I was aware there were a lot of footsteps behind me, and I turned. Fifteen or so people were following me. They intended to bottle me into a corner on one of the side streets.

I turned and began to windmill the nightstick at them, chasing them back to the wagon.

The situation was getting increasingly worse, and as I approached my car, I leaned in long enough to call another *Assist*.

When the dispatcher initiates an assist officer call, every car in the district can go to the scene. Cars from other districts can go, if they are close.

If the dispatcher initiates a *second assist*, indicating the need for additional help, every car in the division can and should go. A second assist is rare.

When I called the second assist, I didn't know that a car from another district, on his way in, arrived on the scene and told the dispatcher the situation was bad and they should consider this a second assist.

So, when I called *my* second assist, I was, in effect, calling a *third assist*.

The dispatcher broadcast: *In the 17th District, at 29th and Tasker, Assist Officer, this is the Third Assist; all Cars Proceed to 29th and Tasker.*

That is an order telling every available car in the city to go. This includes every car, every wagon, every supervisor, every highway patrol car and motorcycle, every burglary team, every ACT team, every Stake Out Team, and anyone else within earshot of the police radio.

There were footbeat men running blocks to get there.

Every available officer in the city was on the way to my location, and the situation was getting worse by the minute. At this point, I estimate there were 1,500 people from the neighborhood crowded in the intersection of 29th and Tasker and in the streets east, west, north, and south of the intersection.

There were fights everywhere. People were running around, screaming, punching at the officers, and the officers were swinging back in turn. Officers hit people who went down and popped back up!

I saw one guy get hit, go down, crawl under a car, come out the other side and haul ass.

There were a few women in the crowd. They were screaming. The men were alternately pulling their kids out or joining in the fight.

I paused for a moment and looked 360°. More people were running toward the fray.

At this point, thinking I was calling the third assist, I reached into the nearest car and called the *fourth assist*.

Veteran officers tell me that was a first.

The biggest assist in the city's history prior to this was a third assist at 2nd and Girard, where several people died, but they couldn't remember a time when there was ever a fourth assist.

I told you I could break anything.

But I didn't *start* this one.

The fights continued as people and officers came running in all four directions toward 29th and Tasker. Looking up and down the four streets from the intersection, all I could see were police vehicles with the lights flashing.

Some officers said they ran more than four blocks to get to the fight because they couldn't get their cars any closer.

Suddenly, as quickly as it started, it stopped.

We were all standing around exhausted, sweating, panting, and looking at one another.

An inspector shouted, "Anyone who doesn't want to be locked up, leave now."

People left the area in various states of urgency.

When it wasn't going fast enough, the inspector shouted, "That's it." and as he pointed to one of the insurgents, "Lock him up."

At once, two officers pounced on the unfortunate draftee and handcuffed him.

As someone moved toward the two officers, the inspector pointed at him and shouted, "Lock *him* up."

This went on for several more iterations until the crowd realized he wasn't kidding, and the pace of egress accelerated. Within a few minutes, most of the people were at least a half block away, but a few were in handcuffs.

In the end, there were nine arrests made. The criteria seemingly being anyone who was bleeding or was among those few slow movers when the inspector decided it was over.

This was to be my one and only riot.

But I didn't start it.

Chapter 51

Bookies: Whatever They Are

There was a fuss about vice, which I could never fully appreciate. Apparently, most of it centered around illegal gambling, the whole issue prompting the commissioner to send us to the 17th District. It centered around video poker machines in bars or something equally cerebral.

Another element of vice, prostitution, was something someone like me couldn't possibly get his head around, but we didn't have any that was visible. My first experience with that was Razzy's arrest, and it was the last until my detective years. That, almost a decade later initiated with Razzy as well, but that's in the next book.

Vice also covered speakeasys, however retro that sounds, and bookmaking.

Keep speakeasys in mind.

I gave up trying to understand bookkeeping in the academy. I never even heard of it until then. Those who were savvy cringed when I asked for details. The instructors thought I was being a smart-ass. I gave up trying to understand because I could see they were getting annoyed.

This was the syndrome manifesting itself. An angry display from others was sometimes required for me to realize that I should stop.

I have no interest nor understanding of social constructs like gambling. If I'm not interested, I drop it.

I don't possess the right wiring for inclusion in the secretive nature of it and, intellectually, it has no upside.

Generally, the more socially intensive something is, the less the chance of my inclusion in it and subsequently understanding it.

The less logically sound something is, the less the chance I'll get involved.

Gambling is a good example.

On this bright sunny morning, however, the bosses decided it was time to send a message to one of the local bookies. The lieutenant called Tom and me. He gave us the following instructions:

"Go to 18th and Federal Streets and stop and question everyone who walks past. If anyone comes out of the store on the corner, stop and question them, too. If they give you any trouble, lock them up."

Dutifully, we went to the corner and started stopping everyone who walked by. We stopped people going to work, people shopping, kids on bikes, the guy delivering papers, and anyone else who showed up.

The store owner came out and said, "Hey, what are you doing here? You're chasing away all my customers."

Yeah, right. Customers came to a *store*, which consisted of a few chairs and an empty counter. We told him to call the lieutenant if he wanted to complain.

When we started stopping cars, however, the lieutenant showed up quickly, laughing, and said, "Get in the car."

He took us back to the district and told everyone in the operations room, "They were even stopping cars."

This was apparently a prelude to raiding the place because about a month later, the lieutenant asked us to come along as he and two other officers served a warrant because we were on that detail.

As we pulled up in front of the store to serve the warrant, the owner came out to greet us.

He said, "What took you so long? We got a call from downtown to expect you two hours ago."

We helped search the place, which was a wasted exercise because I didn't know an illegal number from a banana.

Somebody found something useful, though, because they paraded it around like George with the $2.00 in *It's a Wonderful Life* before handcuffing the owner and taking him in.

Chapter 52

A Speakeasy, Really?

Vice is much less romantic in real life than as characterized in many movies and TV shows. Remember *Miami Vice,* two guys rolling around in Miami in expensive clothes and even more expensive cars? This story gives you a peek into just how sordid it really was.

When I first heard the word *speakeasy* in the academy, I thought it was a reference to an archaic institution from prohibition.

Surprisingly, they were talking about the current time and speakeasys still existed.

Pennsylvania, established by religious groups, enacted some of the most conservative laws in the country concerning the sale and consumption of alcohol.

New York, the drinking age was eighteen, and you could buy alcohol in almost any convenience store.

In the South you could get it in a gas station, convenience store, or Piggly Wiggly supermarket.

In Pennsylvania, the drinking age was twenty-one, and the only proper identification for the sale of liquor was a state-issued Liquor Control Board ID card. Not even a driver's license was sufficient. No LCB card, no alcohol.

Beer, by the case, was only available in a beer distributor or by the six-pack in a bar where the limit was two. Only state-owned and operated State Stores could legally sell wine or liquor.

Bars operated from eight in the morning until two in the morning the next day only, except after-hours clubs, which could stay open until three in the morning.

The state prohibited alcohol sales on Sunday, with the weird exception of Inns, which still existed in the 1970s, distinguished by their integrated restaurants and rooms for rent. There was only one of these I knew, the Blue Bell at the corner of 70th Street and Woodland Avenue.

People developed workarounds, which the state labeled *vice crimes*. One of these was running over to the New Jersey side of the Delaware River to buy untaxed liquor in their commercial liquor stores or down I-95 into the State of Delaware for the same reason.

Liquor in Pennsylvania required a State Tax Stamp Label over the lid, or we would arrest you and confiscate the liquor.

In the inner-city, speakeasys were a popular workaround.

The academy described it thus: The operators of the speakeasys accumulated liquor from assorted sources in assorted-sized containers and held *parties* in their homes after the bars closed.

The party was a ruse to explain why people were in this home drinking off hours. The proprietors of these *speaks*[28] were selling drinks like a bar and charging a substantial markup, usually 200% or more.

They would also sell bottles-to-go, usually the small pint-sized ones you could stick in your pocket.

Some speak owners placed a birthday cake on the dining room table to reinforce the idea of a party, in case the police should happen onto the place.

---

[28] Cop talk for speakeasy.

It was almost impossible to find these places as a uniformed officer unless someone was mad enough at the owner to *drop a dime*[29] on them. We usually didn't know where they were.

One morning at about five, I was relaxing in my car, watching the snowfall. It was a nice respite from the busy nights and incessant radio chatter; in this neighborhood, when it snowed, everything stopped.

Add the early hour, and it was nice and quiet.

The two inches of snow on the sidewalk grew as a nice tranquil display of large flakes floated down on the neighborhood.

The contrast to the normal routine made me realize just how hectic this place was. I was enjoying the dancing snowflakes; police activity the furthest thing from my mind.

Until I noticed movement to my right.

It was a man staggering down the side street. As he came to the corner, he saw the police car, and it got him so rattled he slipped and fell.

I got out to help him up.

When I reached to help him, he recoiled and reached inside his coat. I pushed on his hand, trapping it so he couldn't pull it out. I could feel the bulge under his coat.

I reached in over his hand, expecting a weapon, but it was a pint bottle of gin.

[29] Drop a dime is an archaic expression meaning call the police or otherwise tell on someone. It originated in the time before everyone carried a cell phone, and everyone dropped a dime in a pay-phone to make a call.

I guess he was trying to avoid a pinch for the gin, so he was instinctively hiding it. Or, perhaps he was checking to see if it broke during the fall.

My concern was my safety; I was checking to see if it was a gun.

When I realized what it was, I set it aside and stood him up. A thought hit me. Where did he get the bottle? I checked the bottle. No PA tax stamp. I handcuffed him and put him in the back of my patrol car.

It hit me! He just came from a speak, and left me a trail directly to it! There was no one else on the street. The only footprints in the snow were *his,* leading back up the sidewalk.

I called for my sergeant, who hated speaks, and told him what I found.

He said, "Take a walk up and see what you see."

I walked back in the footprints to a house, which stood out like a Christmas Tree, lit up among the darkened ones surrounding it.

I could hear music and loud conversation through the front windows.

The sergeant was delighted.

He said, "Call for a wagon."

When the wagon arrived, we put my new friend in the back and drove to the house. We knocked on the door, and when a woman opened it, her eyes almost left their sockets.

The sergeant said, "We have a complaint of a disturbance here."

The woman said, "No, we're just having a party."

The sergeant said, "You don't mind if we come in to check, do you?"

She said, "No."

In we went.

There was a nice bar in the dining room where several patrons were loudly discussing *Heisenberg's Uncertainty Principle*. There were couches in the living room against the walls, occupied by others in various states of mumbling inebriation and semi-consciousness.

The best part was a large cake in the middle of the dining room table that was so old, I think Moses put it there when he went up the mountain.

Barely visible on top – Happy Birthday – and a smudge! The name had bled into the once icing, now grey concrete. The icing cracked around the shrunken center, and the candles pointed in every direction.

Long ago, someone poked a finger in the cake, exposing layers now hard as stone.

This prop sat so long it turned to rock. The proprietor was not wasting her profits on new props.

The entrepreneur and her patrons got a ride to the district. We boxed the liquor for confiscation. We hauled away three cases of pint-sized bottles, the stock from behind the bar, and several cases of beer.

Chapter 53

A Prego in the Snow

One of the things I don't miss the most about the Northeast is the weather. Even though it helped us find a speakeasy, I especially don't miss snow. It's not the idea of snow or snow itself, it's the fact once it starts, it seems like it never goes away. Introduce an emergency during a snowstorm, and life gets interesting.

When the winter season starts, and I don't mean the official winter from December 21st to March 19th, I mean the real NE winter starting at the end of October and ending when it feels like it.

Everything is cold all the time, and the sky is constantly gray.

When the snow comes for the first time in fall, it's beautiful, it's fun and a welcome change. At first, you're excited it's snowing, but it starts to stink fast, like fish and visiting relatives.

It would be one thing if you knew when it would start and end, like in Anchorage, where it starts in November, and the ground stays covered until May. That way, you can be prepared for the whole affair, or better yet, choose not to live there.

In Pennsylvania, it is like the sword of Damocles, likely to drop at any time. This is especially bad in February and March when you know spring is coming, but it won't come fast enough.

I was tired of cold, snow, heavy clothing, snow, no sunshine, and snow. February 1978 brought us the worst snowstorm since my childhood. I was driving patrol car 1711 on midnights when it started. It came fast and heavy. By two in the morning, it was pushing six inches.

I like to be prepared; I called the radio dispatcher and asked permission to *"Go to the garage to have chains put on."*

Chains are something you rarely see now because of radial all-weather tires and the fact most cars are either front-wheel drive, all-wheel drive or 4×4.

In 1978, they were all rear-wheel drive, and radials were relatively new. When the snow got over a foot deep, it was almost impossible to get around with rear-wheel drive without snow chains.

I drove to the shop, where they installed a set of chains on my rear tires, and I was good to go. Over the radio, I could hear other cars getting stuck, and by now, everyone was asking to go, so the supervisors created a waiting queue.

In the interim, they were slippin' and slidin' while I was plowing around like a tank.

I answered my calls with no problems, but as 8:00 AM rolled around, a new issue arose. The officers in the early end of the next squad were calling-in because they couldn't get out of their driveways, let alone get to work.

Most officers at the time lived in NE Phila, and the main artery, I-95, was under at least two feet of snow; the plows couldn't keep up. Very few drove Jeeps or 4×4s.

I received an *out-of-district* call, one of the few in my uniform career. The cars in that district either couldn't move, or the district was short-staffed because the relief officers weren't showing up.

The call I got was: *2048 Sigel Street, Hospital Case, Maternity.*

I answered, *"1711, that's the 1ˢᵗ District."*

The dispatcher responded, *"1711, that's correct."*

I answered, *"1711 enroute."*

I threw on the lights and siren, which was funny because although the lights worked fine, all I got from the siren was a sound that reminded me of the distant mewing of a kitten. The storm had packed the horn on the roof with snow.

I continued to Sigel Street, one of those *horse streets* in South Philly which are normally a tight squeeze, but with four feet of drifting snow, was impossible to navigate. The plows, at their best, would hit these streets last, if at all, and with this level of snowfall, they couldn't clear the cross street.

I parked at the corner and plunged those knee-high police-issue snow boots past their tops to the house halfway up the block.

I knocked. The door was immediately answered by a man in his twenties looking like he just saw a ghost. He carried an overnight bag in his hand, and closely behind him was his nine-month-pregnant wife, mouth-breathing like a marathon runner.

He said, "What are we going to do?!"

I looked at him, her, back at him and said, "Carry her."

I said, "Do you know what a fireman's carry is?"

His blank face said, "No." so I told him to go to the pavement. I walked her out the front door, down the three steps, put my arm around her under her arms, and told him to mimic me.

When he did, I squatted, put my arm under her bottom and told him to do the same and grab my arm. When he did, I looked at her and said, "OK?"

She nodded.

I told her, "Sit down."

She sat on our forearms.

I told her husband, "Stand up."

He did, and we stood with her in a cradle created by our arms.

I said, "OK, ready?"

He nodded.

I looked at his wife, and she nodded sideways through the breathing, like a swimmer catching her breath.

We trudged the half-block to the police car and set her down. I opened the back door and motioned for him to get in first. We helped his wife in, and I got behind the wheel.

I started off and notified the dispatcher we were on the way to the hospital. I was taking my time when a blood-curdling scream came from the back seat. I looked in the mirror, and she was screaming and trying to lie down.

I turned the siren back on, throttled up and broke half the chains trying to get to the hospital. The loose links from the chains slashed the side of the car to bare metal.

That would have to wait; we gathered up the expecting mom and carried her into the ER.

This was my first maternity case. I was surprised to see the ER unruffled by the whole thing, even though the woman was still wailing louder than my snow-filled siren.

They casually put her in a wheelchair, took her info, and rolled her to the back, screams and all.

I expected something more dramatic, but they apparently considered childbirth more of a natural event.

I got what I needed from the new dad, returned to my car and drove back to HQ to prepare the report for the damage.

No one seemed to care, and by the time winter was over, almost all the cars showed the same type of damage. The cars remained like that, the damage rusted, and the cars looked nasty until eventually replaced.

And snow never ends. Instead of reporting off as usual that morning, we were all held over for a second shift. Since none of the relief officers could navigate the snow, we worked a double.

Day work was eight hours of trudging through snow, handling accidents, calming frayed tempers, extricating stuck vehicles, unblocking roadways and other activities, rendering us spent, sweat-soaked and ripe when finally relieved.

Luckily, it was the last day of the tour, so I was able to get plenty of sleep afterwards. I spent several hours on gear maintenance after resting: thoroughly cleaning and oiling the revolver, drying and refinishing my rig, and thoroughly drying the boots, leather coat, and fur hat because the white stuff wasn't going anywhere soon.

Clear enough picture about why I don't like snow?

N.B. the official record was 16 inches, but that's *way* off. They must have been measuring in a cylinder somewhere because the reality was perhaps 16 inches in areas where it fell straight down, but the inner city has the added benefit of drifting, so there were areas where it was over 4 feet.

16 inches is still over most car tires, but on the small streets it had drifted up to my knees.

The official date of the storm was February 5 - 7, 1978.

Chapter 54

Mike vs. The World

Mike, the cadet who plunked his revolver on the sill while frequenting the men's room, was a unique individual. He was tall, athletic, and handsome in a way that made girls lose their balance. I call them girls because Mike and I met in high school, and they were still girls.

He always seemed like he was getting ready to be sarcastic, but behind that first glimpse was the smile of someone always happy to see you.

He was an all-around happy person.

The uniqueness in his personality was most apparent when some supervisor tried to punish him. I can't imagine what they would have wanted to punish him for, probably some sharp-tongued remark they didn't like, but it never took.

We were in different squads, so we rarely got to work at the same time, but on this morning, his squad was on day work, and the snowstorm was keeping them from making it in to work. The sergeants from Mike's squad requested volunteers to work an additional shift while the oncoming shift got up to speed as guys trickled in.

Mike made it in because he lived near me in SW Philly, close to the 17th. His sergeant was in the operations room talking with another sergeant about Mike. He was already in a bad temper when I walked up, and when I didn't respond exactly as he expected, he snapped at me with, "Do you *want* to work overtime or *not*?!"

I said, "Yes, sir." to calm him down, but his rotten demeanor was impenetrable.

He and Mike were opposites.

After he dismissed me, he turned to the other sergeant, pointed out the window and said, "Look at him."

I could see Mike through the window, on the sidewalk outside the operations room, throwing a snowball.

The sergeant fumed, "You can't punish him. No matter what you do, he finds a way to turn it around. Last week, I sent him to the bus, and he came back raving about a movie he saw."

"Now, I told him he's off his car and has to walk the footbeat in the snow, and he's out there having fun with the neighborhood kids in a snowball fight."

"I don't know what to do with him."

My thought was, "Leave him alone. You miserable ass."

Consider the malevolence of someone who *insists* on someone being miserable with their punishment. The sergeant was miserable with himself, so he assumed everyone else should be. He was a special kind of wrong.

And, he was someone not bright enough to realize no matter what he does to Mike, Mike will find a way to enjoy it, making *him* miserable instead.

He could have put Mike in a room full of horse manure, and Mike would look for a pony.

Chapter 55

Somebody Gotta Be Last

"You can please some of the people some of the time and all of the people… aw… you know, the thing."

- Definitely not Abraham Lincoln

Sergeant Palmer had a bone to pick with me, so I tried to keep clear of him because every time he got a chance to pick at me, he would. This started with a general distaste for some gear I wore. He didn't cause me a lot of grief; he just didn't like trouble, and I was not the poster child for conformance. His latest beef was when I showed up at a roll call wearing a trooper cap.

This was a Russian soldier-looking fur hat we could wear when the temperature outside went below 32°F. He wanted me to wear the regular uniform hat to roll call and change to the trooper cap after.

This day, thinking he was off, I showed up at roll call with the hat on.

"Mickey!" he hollered, "What did I tell you about that hat?"

"Sorry, sergeant, I thought you were off today," I said.

The group snorted a laugh.

"That don't mean shit," he said. "Don't wear it to roll call whether I'm off or not."

"OK, sir," I said.

"Go change the hat," he ordered.

I ran off and put the normal hat on.

When I got back, he looked over and said, "That's better." "Now, last week, I told everyone to make sure they're not stirring up any trouble. When you go out from here, I want you to find some place to sit. If police radio calls, answer the call and go back and sit some more. Don't go looking for trouble. Now, the captain wants to tell you something. Cleaver, tell the captain we're ready."

Cleaver went into the captain's office.

About ten seconds later, the captain came out of his office to address us.

Now, the captain was, how should I put this short – tempered. Rumor suggested a promise of something in exchange for putting up with us for a year or so, but things weren't going as planned, so he was often in a mood.

He would give it a good effort; he would start out pleasant, but it would go downhill fast.

Today's subject was *activity*. The captain came with a list of it.

He said, "This squad has the lowest activity of any squad in the district. You are lowest in tickets, car-stops, ped-stops, part-one and part-two crimes. Now, I want you to pick up your activity. The numbers look bad downtown, so I want more activity, and I know you can do it. So, get out there and get aggressive."

He looked at the sergeant and said, "Carry on."

We watched as he left the roll call room, went into his office and shut the door.

The sergeant waited until the door shut and turned back to us.

He said, "Somebody gotta be last. Now, remember what I said: go out there and sit. Answer the radio and go back and sit some more. Don't do nothin. *Dismissed.*"

Chapter 56

Rattus-Norvegicus

As I pushed the creaking two-ton police car through the streets of South Philadelphia, I tried to picture my dad leading a team of horses on the same constricted path. I was moving east, and the sun, on its slide to the horizon, was peeking through the rear window; I adjusted my mirror to shield my eyes. I was on the way to Broad Street, where tickets were plentiful, when I noticed an oddly shaped mass of people ahead. I let the dispatcher know I was going to investigate a crowd.

Any time more than a few people would gather, they were *a crowd*.

Crowds have unique personalities.

The spectator crowd moves and cheers as a unit and allows the object of the exercise, usually a fistfight, movement, so the crowd expands and contracts like a swarm of bees, a living moving fog.

The actively fighting crowd, AKA The Mob, has a unique sounding, aggressive roaring noise that rises and falls as the number of participants grows and shrinks.

This crowd was giving off strange vibes with a character all its own. I couldn't quite gauge what they were up to.

They focused as a swarm on something in a corner created by the front wall of a row house and the concrete stairs leading to its first floor. Intermittent shrieks and yelps came from among this odd knot of people. I got out to see what it was.

Two things are an absolute must when you leave the police car: the hat and the stick. Everything else is either attached to the belt or in a pocket.

The hat and stick are separate, unlike the gun and blackjack, so when I got out of the car, I put the hat on and picked up the stick. I carried the stick in my right hand, hanging down to my side. This was ideal because it was somewhat non-threatening, and I could bring it quickly into action.

Normally, when you approach a crowd, they won't move unless you force them to. They want to keep you from getting to the action for as long as possible, usually to allow the action figures to flee. But when I approached this group, they were glad to see me, which was different.

I asked what was going on, and someone exclaimed, "A rat."

As I got closer, I could see it. It was a big one, standing on its hind legs with its back against the wall.

I'm not a fan of cliché, but this was the living and breathing example of two, a cornered rat and a creature with its back to the wall.

What happened next occurred in one uninterrupted movement.

I felt like Moses as I walked into the crowd, and they parted to make way. Anticipation was high as they wondered what I would do. I had no idea, but my stick was at the ready.

I walked through the crowd to the inside edge of the crescent of people around the rat and, without thinking, stepped into the void. The once active and noisy crowd grew apprehensively quiet and shrank back, giving me room.

I stepped into the area in front of the rat – we made eye contact. For a second, we sized each other up, but when I moved closer, I crossed his last awareness zone.

It flew at me as if shot from a cannon, aiming for my neck like the bunny in *Monty Python and the Holy Grail.* I sidestepped, my stick moved in an arc and hit it like an airplane propeller.

I caught it in mid-flight. There was a sickening whack; the rat thudded against the wall and hit the ground, as dead as disco.

The crowd reacted with a roar of "YEAAAAAY." accompanied by an enthusiastic round of backslapping and handshaking.

This startled me more than the rat.

I instantly became an urban legend in that part of the neighborhood. Every time I drove near that corner, someone would see my car, point and tell the story to their friends in vigorous pantomime; I was the cop who killed the rat with his stick. There were open smiles, waves, and sometimes even bows when I passed.

Some people work all their lives to become a legend. All it took for me was one stanky rat.

BTW: The title is from the eidetic memory. We dissected a rat in pharmacy school. The rat's scientific name is: Rattus-norvegicus. The one we did was white: Rattus-norvegicus-albinus.

Another interesting genetic variation.

Chapter 57

There's Streetwise and There's Streetwise.

Tom and I were sitting and exchanging vital information on the island formed by the intersection of Point Breeze, Reed and 21st Street when we heard the shots. We were already racing to 23rd when the dispatcher broadcast *23rd and Reed, Gunshots on the highway.*

We told them we heard the shots and were on our way.

We arrived before the smoke cleared.

There was a young woman on the corner wearing a long winter coat with her hands in her pockets. When she saw us, she urgently pointed at a Cadillac speeding away from the scene south on 23rd.

We were right up his tailpipe.

We pulled him over and, with guns drawn, ordered him out of the car. He complied immediately with his hands up. We frisked him and said, "Where's the gun?"

He exclaimed, "She has it."

We stepped back. It was then we got a good look at his car and the bullet holes.

She was the one with the gun!

He said he was trying to convince her to go with him, and she wouldn't, so he got a little too aggressive. He was in the driver's seat, and he reached out and grabbed her by the arm. He said she pulled a gun from her pocket and started shooting.

There were shards of glass all over the interior of the car where she blew out his left rear window, and there was a bullet hole in the headrest behind his head, another in the passenger side.

As she was shooting, she stepped back and fired a shot through his windshield and another into the back seat. I found one of the bullets on the floor.

Of course, she was gone, and my man did not know her name.

When Sergeant Palmer arrived and we told him the story, he said, "Who has the paperwork?"

"Write it up as UNFOUNDED."

I said, "What? How could it be unfounded? She shot out his windows."

He said, "Did you see it?"

"No." I said, "But we have a witness."

He said, "He's not going to testify."

The man who was within earshot was shaking his head.

I said, "What about the bullet holes in the car?"

He said, "What bullet holes?"

I pointed.

He said, "That could have been caused by anything."

I said, "Yeah, like a bullet."

I showed him the one I found.

He said, "Were did you get that?"

I said, "From the back seat."

He said, "Let me see it."

I handed it to him, and he put it in his pocket.

He said, "Now there's no bullet. Resume, this is unfounded."

That woman was streetwise.

If we were a little less green, we might have at least made a gun pinch.

We would learn.

Chapter 58

Shoot Don't Shoot?

A controversial topic in the news is deadly force. It's the ultimate test of any officer. This chapter sets some groundwork for an actual test presented in the next chapter. What would you do, faced with such a test?

During our training, a lawyer delivered a guest lecture. He was a defense lawyer, so everyone naturally bristled at his presence.

He was there over several days. I mentioned this to a friend. He said, "Yeah, he specializes in defending cops. He was *my* lawyer. Listen to what he says."

I told my classmates about this, so they calmed down about his lectures and paid attention; well, I did.

One of his points stuck: "The gun is for your protection, nothing else. It's for you to protect yourself from deadly force. If you remember this, you'll be OK."

After he left, questions surfaced about some gray areas.

At the time, the Crimes Code permitted the use of deadly force against a fleeing felon. But some non-violent crimes were felonies. Auto theft, for example, as well as retail theft after the second offense or any theft over $2,000. The question was, do we shoot someone fleeing that sort of crime?

The cadre tried to counsel the class on the wisdom of using deadly force against any fleeing felon, not just the previous examples, which, to me, were no-brainers.

Their message was: *"Don't shoot people who are running away."*

When you think literally, things are easy. I felt the lawyer's comment covered the whole subject. If my life wasn't in immediate danger, I wasn't going to shoot.

I once heard a detective say, "If you catch one, you catch them all." His meaning was if you have a group who runs and you catch one of them, they'll tell you who the others are.

Yet, cadets still launched questions at the cadre whenever the issue arose. Some were adamant that the Crimes Code allowed for the use of deadly force against fleeing felons.

One of the instructors possessed a law degree, so the class put it to him. Would *he* ever shoot a fleeing felon?

He said, "If I came upon the scene of a violent felony, where I witnessed the crime myself, and the actor fled, I would first consider the nature of the crime, process what I had seen and consult the Crimes Code."

"I would call my attorney and explain the situation to him. If he agreed I was within my rights to use deadly force, I would sit, smoke a cigarette, have a cup of coffee and decide what to do."

"If, after all of this, and having no other way to catch the fleeing felon, and knew beyond any shadow of a doubt not stopping him would cause mayhem to me, my family, or some other innocent person, and the bad guy was still within range, and there were no innocent bystanders, maybe. Other than that, no."

Chapter 59

Annin Street

Seemingly mundane calls can turn into a shitshow in a split second. During that first year, I received a radio call about a disturbance on the highway that did just that.

The dispatcher sent me to 21st and Annin Streets for a disturbance. I arrived, saw no disturbance and told the dispatcher to release any patrol cars on the way.

There was a sketchy bar on the corner. I pulled into 21st, facing the wrong way, and parked with the curb on the driver's side. The bar was to my left. I was making notes in my log.

An old man approached and said, "They're in the alley."

He was by my left elbow.

I looked at him and said, "Who?"

He pointed, said, "Behind the bar," and walked off.

I could tell by the look on his face he was frightened.

The *alley* was Annin Street. Annin Street was what we referred to as a horse street because when built, horses were the main mode of transportation. Compared to 21st Street, it was an alley. It was actually a very small street behind one row of houses, including the bar on the corner. One of many strange inner-city street configurations.

A car could barely fit, and no cars parked there.

I pulled my car forward a few yards and turned left onto Annin Street, directly behind the bar. It was just getting dark when your eyes are trying to adjust. I heard something to my left in a dilapidated doorless shed at the rear of the bar.

Our cars came equipped with a spotlight on the driver's side left of the windshield. We could aim it from inside the car. I hit the open doorway with a flood of light.

A female voice screamed, "Help, they rapin' me!"

Time froze.

What I saw was surreal, and it took a nanosecond to process. Processing was also going on inside the shed.

Frozen in the beam were three people: a fortyish woman on her back with a young man kneeling between her legs. At her head was another young man, also kneeling, pinning her shoulders to filthy concrete.

And, like someone shouted, *"Action!"* The whole scene sprang to life.

The men scrambled to their feet; I slammed the car into park with the radio receiver in my right hand. My left hand was opening the door as I said, *"1711, 21ˢᵗ and Annin, rape in progress, send back up!"*

I was on the street now and released the receiver, stretched to its coiled wire limit, it slingshotted back into the car.

I drew my revolver as the males scrambled from the shed.

The first ran straight to the adjacent yard through a void in the fence. The other, still struggling to pull up his pants, ran straight into me. I pushed him against a telephone pole just as Herc arrived.

I shouted, "Cuff him!"

Herc cuffed him to the pole, and I went after his partner.

I was running along the outside of the yards, watching him vault fences from yard to yard, when he got to a yard with no exterior fence and broke into the open, east on Annin Street, me behind him.

South on Annin Street was a block-long empty lot where houses once stood. The lot was a neighborhood garden. He knew the path and took off.

I was ten yards behind him when I hit the garden of freshly plowed earth, now a quagmire of mud from a recent rain. It was like running in slow motion.

After ten feet, I knew I couldn't catch him. He took off across that lot like a starship hitting warp speed.

And, the dilemma surfaced. I was chasing someone running from a rape. One of the most heinous crimes on the books, and I saw him doing it. Not someone stealing a car nor ripping off a store.

I still carried my revolver in my hand, I thought, *"This is the worst kind of fleeing felon scenario I can imagine."* He was getting further and further away.

I *could* stop him if I wanted.

But the idea I could probably run faster with the gun in the holster quickly replaced the thought as I snapped it up and redirected my energies to negotiating the quagmire.

He was a half-block ahead; I knew he was going to escape.

He turned with a happy face, knowing he was home free.

When the police wagon pulled into his path.

He turned away from me and plowed face-first into the wagon. The wagon didn't give. He knocked himself silly and fell to the street, where the wagon crew happily scooped him up and handcuffed him.

When I got back to the telephone pole, Herc was there listening to that one plead for Herc to take the handcuffs off so he didn't get a splinter. With his pants still down around his ankles, he was afraid he might get a splinter from the pole.

199

I went to the car to update the dispatcher, who said they were looking for a description of the third male. Apparently, the detectives were right. Each of the males, when approached by the police, gave the other one up so fast it appeared there was one still at large.

Neither one of them knew at this point the other was in custody.

I found out these two were a two-man crime wave when I appeared in court for each of them. The court system separated them because one was a juvenile.

The judge said, "What did I tell you the last time you were here?"

Apparently, they raped an 80-year-old woman two weeks prior to this incident and threw her down a flight of stairs after burglarizing her home.

The complainant on my job was the best, though.

She stood up in court and said, "They was trying to fugg me. If it hadn't been for that officer right there, they woulda fugged me."

She had turned and scanned the courtroom, where there were thirty spectators and at least a dozen other police officers. She pointed directly at me as she testified.

This was a juvenile court, and the judge immediately judged the teen delinquent and sent him directly to a juvenile detention center. The ultimate revolving door. He was seventeen years old.

The other who was nineteen, an adult, didn't fare as well.

Chapter 60

Crime Family

"The family who preys together, stays together."

— The Author

As if the previous team wasn't enough, Herc introduced me to an entire family of bad actors.

The neighborhood I patrolled was so densely populated syndicates often operated within a one block area. The gangs identified by the name of the street, clearly defining their territory. This syndicate was a family in every sense of the word, and they developed a new idea. The idea of having their enforcement done by juveniles.

By enforcement, I mean shootings.

The court system handled juveniles differently from adults. They did not go to prison like adults. The most the court could do was judge them delinquent and send them to a minimum-security juvenile facility or camp, from which they often walked away. And, when they turned eighteen, the courts sealed their criminal records. They got a clean slate.

Herc pointed out one particularly heinous individual and told me an unbelievable story.

The gang chose this kid, who was now fifteen, to start shooting people at twelve years old. They gave him a gun in a brown paper bag, pointed out victims and dropped him off a block away. He walked to where the victim stood and, as he was passing behind him, shot him in the head right through the bag.

Herc said he did this for several years undetected. We finally caught him in the act, but since he was fifteen, juvenile court released him into the custody of his parents. Parents was a loose term; the only one at home was his mother. His father was serving time in the state prison for another murder. It was indeed a family business.

We stopped to talk to this kid. He was unflappable. Herc introduced me. The kid pointed to my shooting badge and asked what it was. Herc explained it was for being a good shot with a handgun.

He grinned and said, "They should give me one of those."

One night on midnights, I was on patrol in the same area when I did something I've found most normal people don't do, look up. I looked up when a flash of light caught my eye in a warehouse. A warehouse that's normally dark at this hour.

I got out of my car and took up a position across the street below a third-floor window when the same kid's face appeared. Seeing me, he quickly drew away from the window, and shortly thereafter, the light went off.

I called for the sergeant and told him what I saw.

He said, "Are you sure you saw someone?"

I said, "I'm not only sure, I know who he is."

The sergeant called for a wagon crew and told the dispatcher to send a K-9 unit. That's cop talk for a *canine unit*, a police officer with a huge German Shepherd partner.

The wagon crew, the sergeant, and I covered the exits to the building until the K-9 unit arrived. The K-9 officer went in with his dog and returned a few minutes later with three youngsters.

It was not only the kid I knew but his thirteen-year-old brother. With them was a twelve-year-old girl. I pulled her to the side and asked her what she was doing with them. She said they initially asked her to come into the building with the promise of some sort of gift.

She continued; by the time they got her to the third floor, it was obvious to her they intended to have sex with her and, despite her objections, had just removed her pants when the older one heard the police car outside putting a stop to the whole thing.

We arrested the two juveniles for burglary and attempted rape, but within a week, I saw the older one walking down the street. Thinking he escaped, I stopped him only to find out they released him to visit his mom for Thanksgiving.

By the time I left the 17th, however, fate finally caught up with him. At sixteen, he committed another homicide, and this time, there were witnesses. A newly passed law treated him as an adult.

He went to the same prison as his father.

Chapter 61

Comp-Clinic Primer

The 17th was a laugh a minute. The people who lived there called it Dodge City for a reason. There was always something happening, and we were always busy. Tonight would bring a new experience.

A handful of us found ourselves involved in a fight on Point Breeze Avenue, involving an argument among the locals turned violent. My sergeant was there directing things.

One individual was particularly rambunctious, and the sergeant said, "Lock him up."

During the struggle with the several officers who were trying to handcuff him, I reached in to help, and the guy bit my wrist. Someone punched him to make him let go. A wagon crew handcuffed him.

I told the sergeant, "He bit me."

The chaos was such that he didn't hear me, so I went back to what I was doing. The officer who punched the prisoner told the sergeant the guy bit me, so when we got inside, the sergeant was upset with me.

He said, "Why didn't you tell me that guy bit you?"

I said, "I did."

He said, "No, you didn't. See the corporal, go to the *comp-clinic*."

I thought of saying something else but thought better of it. Off to the comp-clinic I went. I was now in IOD status (Injured on Duty).

The comp-clinic, short for compensation clinic, only operated during normal working hours. An officer drove me to the ER. Nurses cleaned the wound, or boo-boo, as they laughingly characterized it, and the doctor released me with the order, *"See the comp-clinic in the morning."*

This was the routine: if hurt off-hours, after treatment in the ER, assuming you were ambulatory, you followed up with the comp-clinic in the morning. The comp-clinic was on the third floor of the same hospital. If your injury was severe, you went to the nearest hospital. Boo-boos went to the specific hospital housing the comp-clinic.

I wasn't prepared for the comp-clinic circus. When I walked in, it looked like any free clinic except not as aesthetically pleasing. I stared at a long hall of orange plastic chairs filled with every recently injured city employee. All city employees, if injured while at work, went to see the doctors in the comp-clinic.

I was looking for a spot among the sanitation and maintenance workers when I noticed someone I knew.

I spotted a female officer, one of *our girls* from the academy. She worked in a district in another part of the city. I was glad to see her, but not about the deep vertical scratches on her face.

She told me that some woman had dug her nails into her face the previous evening. We experienced simultaneous assaults.

I was not at all upset by my bite marks, but I was more than upset with the long cuts on her fresh, young face. There were at least three, if not four, long scratches along her cheeks on either side of her bright blue eyes.

I said, "What happened to the person who did this?"

She said, "She's in the hospital."

"Good," I said. "Are you OK?"

She said she was, but I could see the concern. Imagine someone disfiguring the face of a twenty-year-old in the first year on the job. Her concern was they would be permanent.

Little did I know that it would soon be my turn.

Chapter 62

Temple Girls

I keep seeing news stories where some politician is asking, "Why does anyone need a gun that holds 15 bullets?" Keep reading.

When called to the police department, I was still attending Temple University, pursuing an accounting degree. One might think, "Oh, a break from police work." Not today.

I tried to fit my school schedule into our rotating work schedule, and Temple was flexible. Some daytime instructors held night classes, so you could attend their day or night sessions. But it was hard not to miss a class or classes during the month.

I scheduled all my classes for Tuesdays and Thursdays. That meant a full day on campus.

On these days, I would bring a cooler in my car with my lunch. I brought my own lunch to save money and my stomach lining. I could also pile all my textbooks in the trunk and change out, so I didn't have to carry all of them.

On this day I was walking to my car parked on Diamond Street, several blocks from the main campus.

I noticed a curious scene, like where a lion is creeping through the tall grass stalking zebras. The thing Snoopy mimics when he creeps up on Lucy.

Two young women, obviously students, were walking to their car parked on a side street. They were busy talking to each other, oblivious to their surroundings. On the side where they parked, was a vacant lot with six-foot-high grass, on the other side a low-rise housing project.

Two men stalked them as they walked. The men were confident, walking in the middle of the street, but their heads were on a swivel. The demonstrative body language was what got my attention.

I carried a five-shot .38 Special revolver, a relatively small gun, on the inside of my left ankle. Not the ideal carry situation, but the idea was concealment because I was in college, and many students didn't react well to guns.

There was a nice big tree beside me, and I was trying to decide if I should hide behind the tree and watch or intervene early.

If I waited until they attacked the students, I would have a shitshow on my hands. I would have to fight with them and, depending on what they were carrying, perhaps shoot one or both.

If I intervened now, I could detain them long enough for the students to get safely away, but would precipitate the *"Why us?"* scenario.

I was also in the middle of the street as these thoughts went through my head.

Keep in mind that this whole thing transpired in less than two minutes, from the time I first saw them 'til it was over.

Well, I didn't have to make the decision because, as I said, their heads were on a swivel. One of them caught me in his periphery, reached over and stopped the other. They froze – then turned.

One did that movement where he raised his shoulders and dropped them while flapping his arms, showing his displeasure. It was the movement Stallone would give me when my joke caused the re-take of the final scene in Rocky II.

I interrupted his plans – he was upset.

As this was happening, the students reached their car.

This is when AS is a benefit. They got no indication of what my intentions were or anything. No input. They stood there for a few seconds, looking at me.

They gave me the NASA salute. That shrugging signal that meant, "What?" "What are you looking at me for?"

I continued to stand motionless in the street. No one can do this like an Aspie. I was like a statue. Their body language showed disgust that I ruined their plan.

Both the students were fumbling for car keys in a purse.

I could have simply walked away, but the two predators were having a short conversation. They began to walk toward me.

As they got within shouting range, the one said, "What are you looking at?"

I always liked this question.

"You," I responded.

He said, "What?"

I repeated, "You, I'm looking right at you."

He got angry.

He said, "You think we were going to do something to those young girls."

I replied, "Shakespeare was right, a guilty conscience needs no accuser."

"Conscience doth make cowards of us all. A wicked conscience mouldeth goblins swift as frenzy thoughts."

To which he responded, "Huh?"

I added, "I said nothing of my thoughts. Your conscience made the accusations."

Of course, this, as usual, pissed them off. Because I have a way of making it obvious, I was using the plural you. My mocking tone helped it along.

A step to my left was a parked car. Cars at this time came with protruding bumpers, bumpers you could put your foot on to tie your shoe.

These two moved and acted as one like we did.

As one, they stepped toward me.

I took a half step to the left and laid my books on the trunk of the car. I put my left foot on the bumper and pinched up my pant leg, exposing the revolver.

It was stainless steel, highly visible. At the sight of the revolver, with my right hand on it by now, both stopped and took two steps back. They needed swivel room to run if necessary.

The students were finally pulling out and driving off, oblivious to what they avoided. Bless their hearts.

The bad guys looked at me, showed me their palms, and said, "No problem." They quickly turned and walked away.

I watched them leave, and when I felt they were a safe distance away. I went back to class. I didn't go to my car; I didn't want them to see which one was mine.

Hours later, as I was leaving class and returning to my car, they were waiting for me. I could see them a half-block away on the corner with friends.

They positioned themselves to cover four directions of approach. When they saw me, there was a sudden communal body movement as they indicated to the others, I was the one.

Six of the group scurried into a nearby doorway, leaving one on the walkway as the decoy. They didn't know the revolver was now in my pants pocket, and as I approached the decoy with my books in my left hand, my right gripped the revolver.

The decoy moved to block my way. The others, armed with crowbars, hammers, tire irons and long flathead screwdrivers, watched from the doorway.

The combination of AS and my appearance was something that made it hard to spot me as a cop. I assume they didn't think they were going to take a police officer's gun; I can't imagine who they thought I was.

I approached their friend on the sidewalk. I mentioned he moved to block the sidewalk, so I stopped in front of him. I looked at him and shot a glance at his droogs in the doorway. They tried to get smaller by huddling closer together, a move I always found amusing.

I looked at the guy in the path.

He said, "Got a match?"

My instinct was to say, *"Yes, my ass and your face."*

But I kept my composure.

I simply said, "No."

He said, "What about a dime? Do you got a dime?"

I said, "No."

He turned and looked at his droogs.

I was supposed to have diverted my attention to fishing out the dime so he could punch me, and the group would wolfpack me and take the gun.

The rest of the group was still trying to hide. They were terrible at it.

I said, "Not going according to script, huh?"

He said, "Huh?"

I repeated, "It's not going according to plan, is it?"

He looked at me frozen. He was afraid. I could see it in his eyes.

I said, "So?"

He stepped out of the way and let me pass.

I looked at the guys in the doorway one last time and shrugged.

I started to cross Diamond Street on a diagonal.

One shouted, "He's got something on his leg."

I stopped, "You sound like you want to come out and see what it is."

He shouted, "I *know* what it is."

I stood there for a few seconds, waiting to see what they were going to do. None of them moved toward me, so I went and picked up my car. I knew I could never park there again.

I drove directly to my favorite gun store and bought a 9mm automatic pistol with a capacity of 15 rounds.

It was to be a prudent decision.

Chapter 63

More Than Hippies
Meet on South Street

Flummox, verb perplex (someone) greatly, bewilder. That's what this call did!

Flummoxed at the scene in front of me, I responded to the second in a series of assist officer calls. We didn't receive the initial *fight in the bar* call because it was in the adjoining district. When the first officer arrived and entered, someone inside locked the door behind him. This area was known for fighting with the police.

I responded to the first assist, but by the time I arrived, the sergeant was waving us off and telling the dispatcher to resume everyone. I knew in my bones it wasn't over, so I sat a block away. I didn't have to wait long. The second call came out two minutes later, and I swung around onto South Street. The flummoxing scene was acting itself out in the middle of the street.

There was a young man in the street; he was about twenty-two. He held the long blond hair of a woman, who appeared to be in her forties, firmly gripped in his left hand. He repeatedly punched her in the face with his right.

He hit her two or three times hard before I could intervene.

I threw the patrol car into park, making a loud rutsching sound as the ratchet gear tried to stop the 4,000-pound beast. This technique allowed me to remove the key and be out of the car before it came to a complete stop.

The male ran into a nearby row house. He got in as I reached the top of the few steps leading to the front door, and he slammed it shut in my face. I pushed against it, but he put his back against the wall opposite the door and placed his feet against the door; I couldn't push it open.

I tried for a few more seconds and noticed there was a window to the left, accessible from the stairs. I went to the window to see where he was. There was only a screen in the window, so I started to remove the screen.

When he saw this, he came to the window, and as I removed the screen, he leaned out and stabbed me in the face just under my right eye.

I shouted, "He just stabbed me."

The sergeant shouted, "Take the door!"

Another officer and I started to kick the door, but the stabber resumed his position against the wall, and the door wouldn't budge.

Someone shouted, "Get the axe."

An officer came running from a wagon with a fire axe and as he topped the steps, shouted, "Get out of the way."

I snatched the axe from his hands. I raised it over my head as the two other officers on the landing dove over the rail to the safety of the sidewalk.

For the next minute, there was no sound but an axe-chopping door. I hit it a few times and concentrated on one of the raised panels, which splintered.

The officer next to me said, "Stop."

He reached through the hole I created to unlock the door. The bad guy grabbed his wrist from the inside and pulled, raking it across the nails sticking from the stiles I had exposed with the axe, opening the officer's arm with long cuts from his wrist to elbow.

I hit the actor in the stomach with my nightstick by poking it through the hole in the door. He grabbed the stick. The officer next to me used his stick to poke him in the face, and he let my stick go, running into the house's interior. It took us a few seconds to unlock the door and run in to find him.

I heard someone outside shout, "We got him!"

Two highway officers caught him in the backyard as he jumped from the second-floor window.

He went to the nearest hospital, and I went to the comp-clinic.

The officers who took him to the hospital continued to restrain him because he started hitting the staff. A nurse and the doctor both punched him.

I went home with a patched-up face and an appointment for the next morning. When the doctor read the report the next morning and removed the bandage, he started cursing.

Chapter 64

Mensch!

As I lay on the gurney, staring at the overhead light, the doctor, a German, assumed I didn't understand him. He was cursing the doctor who put the patch on my face the previous evening.

He called for a nurse and ordered a plastic surgery kit.

He spent the next hour putting small stitches in my face so I wouldn't scar.

He muttered the whole time, "This third-world jackass from the ER. It might be OK for people from his country to walk around with scars, but to make a twenty-three-year-old man live the rest of his life with a scar on his face is criminal."

(Actually, he said "unglaublich sein.", which doesn't come across literally well; what he meant in this context was criminal.)

He pressed the flesh back into place with such force I thought he would push my head through the gurney. He cursed and swore and stitched and daubed till satisfied there would be no scar.

I left with one hell of a shiner, but the work he did was fantastic.

He instructed me to come back to him for the removal of the stitches and insisted I not let anyone else take them out.

He said, "When you are old, and your skin sags, you might see a scar. But until then, you will see nothing when it's fully healed."

He was right. Even now, I must intentionally look for it, and I know where it is.

Thank God he took his oath seriously.

When it was time for court, I got a call from a local politician.

Our bad guy was now clean and sober, and he and his mom, the woman he was punching, had reconciled. With no prior record, he wanted my OK to put him into a program where he would plead guilty but, upon the completion of some years of probation, would allow for the expungement of his record.

With the promise of a future favor from the politician, I agreed.

I put the favor in the bank and carried on.

Chapter 65

Allow Me to Introduce You to my Friend Mace

"I learned this trick from Ed."

— The Author

It was a weekend, a real weekend, which is something we waited a month for. It was a Saturday in the summertime, and I was on my RDO, equipped with money, a car and the desire to drive to the seashore.

My sister had acquired a place in Sea Isle City, NJ, which she was renovating to flip.

She said, "Come down for the weekend." so I did.

I drove down Springfield Avenue on my way to the Ben Franklin Bridge. But when I got to 57th Street, barricades blocked my route. There was a bodacious block party in progress. There was no alternative but to go around it.

Springfield Avenue is one of the safe passage arteries crossing West Philly. Philly is a city of neighborhoods. When passing through someone else's neighborhood, everyone knew to keep your arms, your eyes, and everything else inside the windows of your car. No one would bother you as long as you stayed on the agreed-upon streets, kept to yourself and kept going.

I needed an alternative route. I could go up to Woodland Avenue, which was the next quasi-safe passage street, but the rules there were not as solid, so I figured I could circumnavigate the block party by holding my breath, moving one street to the left, quickly passing through the side-street, and back onto the avenue.

I thought, I am the man, so I'll be OK.

At that time, New Jersey law prohibited outside police officers from carrying guns. I left mine at home. As it is one of the major badges of office, I felt a little naked as I turned.

I made it all the way through the side street and was approaching the stop sign when I realized it wasn't going exactly as I'd planned. There were two young men walking on 56th Street about to cross. They saw me and, for all intents and purposes, jumped into the intersection in front of my car to trap me. So, they thought.

I waited as they strutted slowly across the street. This was a common provocative action in the big city.

As they did this, I kept eye contact with them because that's what men do. They stopped in front of the car. I sat and waited to see what they were going to do.

I figured they should allow this minor break in protocol, since they did have the whole f-ing block of Springfield Avenue blocked for their soiree.

But they were determined not to let me pass without displaying umbrage. *Umbrage* is the university word. Retelling later in the locker room it was *peacocking*.

One went to the sidewalk while the other stood in front of my car and continued to grit on me. I waited patiently for him to get tired of the whole affair when he said, "What are you looking at?"

Creative, no?

I said, "You, I'm looking at you."

He said, "What?"

I said, "Did I stutter? I'm looking at you. I'm looking *right at* you."

He couldn't believe my brass. I could see the one on the sidewalk beginning to bristle and move toward the car.

The one in the front came running to the driver's side window and lunged at me. Since I couldn't take a gun, I kept a mace canister on my sun visor. I hit him in the face with a blast of liquid tear gas.

He immediately withdrew with shouts of, "Pussy! You mother fucker!"

That's when the other decided it would be prudent for him to back up his friend with the same approach and the same results.

So, I zapped him.

Apparently, this stuff smarts because when they backed away from the car, they both tripped backwards over the curb and were now firmly on their prats, rolling around cursing, shouting, and calling me every name in the book.

"Pussy, mother fucker." they shouted in unison.

I said, "What did you say? I can't hear you." as I continued to hose them down until the can sputtered and died as the final drops landed. I shook the can and tried again, but it was bone dry.

I said, "Here, you can have this now." and threw the can, hitting one in the head.

Then I took a right, turned left back onto Springfield Avenue, and drove down to the seashore.

I stopped for burger along Rt. 130 on the way and enjoyed two burgers, fries, and a large coke, the mandatory start to any good seashore adventure.

I wonder how my friends spent the rest of their day.

I love the seashore.

Chapter 66

Cry Havoc and
Let Slip the Dogs of War!

Tired of the infiltration of the other district's burglary teams, I took advantage of the next incident to teach one a lesson.

As summer bloomed in 1978, the dispatcher broadcast an *assist officer call* at 20th and Pt. Breeze. When I arrived, there was a crowd of about 20 civilians and four or five officers. As the sergeant pulled up, he told the dispatcher there were enough cars on the scene. I jumped out right behind him.

Randall was in the middle of the island at that intersection, with his stick out, dueling with a bad guy with a machete. I found myself wondering if he might not want to think of some other weapon to use when another officer blindsided the guy with his stick across the wrist and knocked the machete to the ground.

A few other officers helped Randall handcuff the guy and put him in a wagon. I was standing next to the sergeant when a group of people started screaming, "You can't lock him up."

I was to see this a lot in the coming days, this was just the first.

Some districts kept a book of sayings along this theme. *"You can't lock him up, he's my brother." "You can't lock him up; he's my cousin."* There were endless variations.

But anyway, this bunch were shouting, "You can't lock him up ...." And one started to push one of the officers.

221

Now, since it was an assist call, the other districts, burglary teams included, came in.

At this point, there were three or four officers wrestling with this guy who was screaming and trying to get away from them. They were right in front of the sergeant and me. The guy was kicking, screaming, punching and doing everything he could to get away.

The sergeant said, "Lock him up."

He fought all the harder, and I couldn't help wondering if there wasn't a better way. I mean, they gave us all these tools to use and yet, these guys were all wrestling with this guy. He was kicking them in the shins and shoulder-butting them, trying to get loose.

It was as bad as Randall and the machete.

I was doing this thing I did: running scenarios. *"What is the best way to control someone, given a certain situation?" "What is the best weapon to use when someone swings at you, punches you, grabs you by the arm?"*

This is an Aspie thing, running every possible scenario through my head to find a solution to a problem.

The training at the academy was thin when it came to the hand weapons they issued us. There was no real instruction on how or when to use them or which ones to use.

We were issued a blackjack. I think the idea was you would put your hand around the spring part and have the strap around the front of your knuckles. That way, it protected your knuckles and kept the lead from springing back and breaking your wrist. That's about the best I could figure since there were no instructions with the thing, and the training wasn't much help.

We carried the blackjack in a special pocket sewn into the right pants leg of our uniform pants. It was about the level of where your hand hung by your side.

I was running through all of this in my mind and was watching the continuing battle in front of me when the guy the officers were still fighting *bit* one of the officers.

I shouted, "Havoc!"

Before I knew it, Jack was out of my pocket and in my hand. It came up over my right shoulder in a spinning arc and landed smack in the middle of this guy's forehead.

This is what this thing was for. Close combat when the stick was useless, and the gun was unnecessary.

At the instant Jack hit the guy's head, the D cell flashlight the sergeant always carried came zipping in a similar arc and whacked the guy also. In a wild frenzy, the wrestling match turned into a slug-fest.

When I hit the guy, it was like ice breaking. No one else was sure what to do either. When I nailed the guy, everyone else seemed to get the message they didn't have to keep taking the kicks and punches, no less human bites.

They must have seen my strike as an indication of what those tools were for.

As soon as I hit the guy, the team pulled him away. It also was the first time I saw this type of situation as well. An older officer I knew warned me about these frenzies where officers accidentally hit one another, but he was now out of my reach.

Knocked to the ground, a burglary team officer was holding him down with his hands behind his back.

He looked up at me and said, "Give me your handcuffs."

I was ready for this.

I said, "Mine are already on someone."

I was glad now. I always carried mine in a case, so he couldn't tell if I was telling the truth or not. Not that it mattered. He wasn't getting my handcuffs.

He hit the guy; he was his prisoner. He must stand him up in court with the hospital helmet next week.

This was yet another example of these outside units trying to bag us with something. He knew he hit the guy last. It was his problem. He was trying to pawn it off on me. Not today.

He kept griping about having to take this prisoner. He felt that he could hit and run. It was apparently beneath him to have to arrest this clown. Bagged by his own trick, he was stuck.

The sergeant asked, "Who hit this guy? Did you hit him?"

He looked at me and said, "Did you hit this guy?"

I said, "No, did you?"

He looked at me funny and said, "No."

All the while, he was tapping his flashlight and cursing. Damn bulb, stupid flashlight. Apparently, since these flashlights were relatively new, they hadn't perfected the bulbs. The bulbs broke when you struck something hard with them. Kind of a design flaw for a police flashlight.

Cops will hit you with just about anything in the heat of battle. I guess that's why there was a compartment in the bottom of the flashlight with an extra bulb in it. You needed it.

We never saw that burglary team again.

Chapter 67

The Magic Memo

"If you're the smartest person in the room, you're in the wrong room."

— Confucius

A statistic I remember from management training was that 60% of business is social and 40% technical. Coincidently, I recently read that 60% of Aspies are unemployed, and 40% are employed in pedestrian jobs.

Since this book is anecdotal vs technical, I'm not going to belabor the point of the reliability of data studies and sources for articles. That subject requires a year to research and its own book.

But I can tell you this for sure: If you are the smartest person in the room, with weak or non-existent social skills, few people line up to hang out with you.

Think, Mr. Spock.

I got a better understanding of this after my diagnosis, and among other things, as quoted in my first book, "I understood why most teachers hated me, and those few special ones treasured me."

The same dichotomy developed early in the department.

This next anecdote is chum for any young psychoanalyst and full of subplots, drama and intrigue.

A group of us rookies were in the detective division after an incident that ended with a half-dozen people under arrest. The detectives already disliked us, a feeling rapidly becoming mutual as we got to know one another.

The first drama: The detective sergeant announced, "Ok, all of you write a memo about what happened."

We found memo forms and started writing. I went to a nearby typewriter, which each detective division has littered around the squad room, and prepared mine.

There was a format for memos taught at the academy. I called up the picture inside my head. It was basic, so I properly formatted one, typed my story, and handed it to the assigned detective.

He read it, physically reacted and bellowed, "What are you, a *college boy?*"

I never heard this in real life, only in the movies.

I said, "Yes, I've been to college."

He scoffed, "Yeah, I thought so." and walked off with the memo.

Apparently, the word college was pejorative in his personal vernacular.

End drama number one.

I was standing looking out the window (fixating, as one of my friends used to call it) when I felt a tug on my right sleeve. I looked to find one of my fellow rookies holding a memo.

He said softly, "Can you look at my memo and see if it's OK?"

I said, "Sure."

I read it. A picture came to mind of a child with a crayon. I could kind of make out the storyline because I was there; he riddled it with misspellings and no sense of grammar or punctuation at all.

I remember this moment often as the first time the voice inside my head said, *"What the hell have I done to myself now?"*

I looked at my man and said, "Yes, it's fine."

Thanking God for the flat affect.

He beamed, smiled and said, "Thanks." and proudly took his memo to the detective. Oddly, the detective seemed more pleased with his.

The second drama: One of the other rookies approached the officer who showed me the memo and chastised him for talking to me at all, let alone letting me proof his memo.

His view was no one could be friendly with me and him at the same time. This fellow was the leader of the clique. He was pulling the memo writer back in line.

His hold over him was strong; the one with the memo never spoke to me again.

As I saw dichotomy morph into trichotomy, I began to accumulate things, people, and places to avoid, and this individual took a position at the top of the list. No matter where we were, no matter what the circumstance, on duty or off, he said something negative and denigrating.

The final drama: My sergeant approached the detective and said, "Is there a problem with his memo?"

The detective said, "No, it's just that…"

The sergeant cut him off, "Let me read it."

He read the memo, looked at me in a whole new way, and handed it back to the detective.

He addressed us rookies as a group, "Finish up here and resume patrol."

"Yes, sir," we replied; he turned and left.

My relationship with my sergeant was about to change.

Chapter 68

Ed's Photos

One of the amazing things Ed did was identify people on the street from their photos. Friends in the department's criminal records department and other contacts provided him with photos of bad guys. He would get mug shots of wanted people in the district and memorize their faces. On more than one occasion, he would recognize them on the street and snatch them up.

I was backing up Randall with a ped-stop, watching his back as he got the man's information so he could run him through the computer. Ed rolled up. We would always get close by one another in case something kicked off.

He was still in his patrol car by the curb when Randall moved his body enough so Ed got a clear view of his ped-stop, sitting in his car. His eyes popped, and he jumped out.

He ran to Randall and said, "Hey, do you know who this is? It's Joe Exitus. He's wanted for homicide."

Randall said, "That's not the name he gave me."

Ed and I looked at each other.

Ed said, "I don't care what name he gave you; his real name is Joe Exitus, and he's wanted. I have a picture in my car."

Ed got the picture.

He held it next to the guy's face and said, "See, it's him."

Randall said, "It doesn't look like him."

Ed looked at me.

I said, "To be honest, I don't see it either."

Ed, frustrated, said, "Look, its Joe Exitus, I'm sure of it."

The radio dispatcher called Randall with response to his inquiry about the fake name the ped-stop provided.

He stepped out of his car and said, "He's not wanted." And told the guy he could go.

Ed said, "Look, I'm sure he's Joe Exitus. If you don't want him, I'll take him."

Randall said, "You can have him."

Ed quickly put handcuffs on him and put him in the backseat of his car, saying to me, "Keep an eye on him, will you?"

Ed was talking to a wagon crew who just arrived when the ped-stop started banging his head on the car window. I motioned for him to stop it until I realized he was trying to get my attention.

I opened the door.

He said, "I am Joe Exitus. I want you to know now so you don't get mad."

I shouted, "Ed."

Ed came running over.

I said, "Tell him."

He looked at Ed and said, "I'm Joe Exitus."

Ed said, "Don't say anything else." and shut the door.

Randall was gone, so Ed put Joe in the wagon and took him in.

I thought, *"Damn, well done. I wish I had that skill."*

Well, shortly thereafter, the dispatcher ordered me to headquarters, where the sergeant's pants were in a wad.

He said, "Were you there for Randall's ped-stop?"

I said, "Yes, sir. Nice pinch."

He said, "Randall complained that Ed stole his pinch, so I'm preparing paperwork. I'll need your side."

I reacted physically, which shocked him.

I said, "Papers for what?"

"To take Ed to the front for stealing the pinch."

"Woah," I said. "If anything, you should be preparing papers for a commendation."

He said, "What?"

I told my side of the story, how Ed told Randall who the guy was and tried repeatedly to convince him, going to the point of showing him a picture. I told him Randall could not be convinced and was letting the guy go and Ed asked him if he minded if he took him since he clearly didn't want him.

The sergeant took a step back. He said, "Really?"

"Really. Randall is lying to you." I told him.

Well, I don't know what happened to Randall, if anything, but the sergeant told me he put Ed in for the commendation and called downtown to validate it was indeed Joe Exitus Ed identified.

Another one of those things I couldn't reconcile. Ed took it in stride, too.

I would have confronted Randall, which would not have gone well for either of us.

Chapter 69

Sammy Smith AKA:
Anwar Abdul Wizbang

Sammy Smith was a low-level drug dealer who lived in a row house in the 17th. He, when it suited him, also went by Anwar Abdul Wizbang.

I mentioned the one call we blew on the first night in the 17th. This was the call.

Sammy sold bottles of prescription strength cough syrup from his crib. His crew would burglarize pharmacies and steal gallon stock bottles of Syrup, its street name, which contained codeine. They would also steal cases of eight-ounce prescription bottles.

They would fill the eight-ounce bottles from the stock bottle and sell the Syrup at $5.00 a bottle in the vestibule of Sammy's house.

The first week we arrived on the 17th, there was a cluster at the Jones residence.

Normally, Syrup customers would knock on the front door, and Sammy, or one of his minions, would invite them into the vestibule. They would collect $5.00 and admit them to the living room. There, they would give them a bottle of Syrup.

The customer would drink the whole thing, and it would create such a high blood level of codeine their body would react to it with an enormous high lasting about 20 minutes. Then, they would kick them out.

This one night, Joe Bad came to the door, and one of Sammy's minions let him in. This minion got confused about how the deal worked and let Joe into the living room. There was a bottle of Syrup on the table for Joe, and the minion went to get Sammy.

When Sammy and the minion returned, Joe had already wolfed down the Syrup and was high on the couch. Sammy asked him for his money and he confessed he didn't have any. Sammy got mad and started slapping him around.

They threw him out the front door with instructions to "Bring back the money."

He came back with a gun. Since he was still high, Sammy and his minion easily wrestled the gun away from Joe. At this point, Sammy was so mad he strangled Joe with his own scarf.

Now, the problem is a dead guy in his living room.

He devised a plan.

Sammy went into the backyard and kicked his kitchen door in. He got two of his minions to hold Joe up in the doorway while Sammy shot Joe a few times with his own gun.

This is a bad day for Joe. First, he's strangled with his own scarf and now shot with his own gun.

Part two of the plan was to call 911 and tell the police you just shot an intruder kicking in your back door. The police will come, and Sammy and the minions are going to tell him they were sitting in the living room watching *Gilligan* when someone with a gun broke through the back door. Sammy grabbed the burglar's gun and shot him.

Good plan, huh?

Here's the onion.

When the dispatcher broadcasts the call, it's in the period when the old 17th and new 17th are changing guard. The old squad has already gone, and the new ones haven't arrived yet. Radio is getting covering chatter from someone in one of the other districts in the division, so the guys who have left don't get into trouble.

You see, the calls didn't stop coming in just because the guys who left were not there to answer them.

Officers who hear an unanswered call for one of their friends answer the call with their friend's car number. They do this because missing a call gets you into trouble. They figure it's probably bull shit anyway, which many of these calls are.

After a while someone comes back on the radio and says the call is unfounded, and no one shows up at Sammy's house.

After about 15 minutes and no police, Sammy and the minions call again. The same thing happens.

They called again at 1:00 AM, and one of the new 17th District rookies got the call. He couldn't find the street. Another call at 2:00 AM went unanswered.

One of the academy supervisors on the street finally picked up the radio and said this call was obviously unfounded, so the dispatcher should disregard any more calls from the address.

Decisive for sure, but not thoroughly thought through.

So, throughout the night, Sammy and the boys are trying to figure out what has happened to their plan. Why haven't the police arrived so they can tell their story?

During the night, they are constantly upgrading their story and rearranging the crime scene. At some point, hiding Joe's scarf behind the couch in the living room. In the meantime, Joe is fermenting in the backyard with bullet holes in his chest and a big wheal around his neck from the scarf.

Sammy and the boys are alternately napping, conspiring and getting high on their own supply. At 9:00 AM the next morning, they decide to try 911 again. But, instead of saying they've been calling on and off all night, they go right into the there's-a-guy-at-my-back-door story.

A new shift is on, and this time, the officers who get the call show up. Sammy is in the middle of his story when an officer who was a medic in the army notices the newly dispatched Joe is as cold as a popsicle.

Homicide detectives get involved. It took about ten minutes for one of the minions to fold. Sammy *hit the books*[30] for homicide.

Sammy gets bail and vamooses down South. There are months of GRMs (General Radio Memorandums: police-radio-commercials) detailing the warrant for Sammy's arrest.

Wanted in the 17th District for homicide, Sammy Smith, male, 24 years, etc., etc.

Now, I happened to be at homicide while the detectives were first questioning him. I was listening to the story, thinking, what a cluster. Sammy sat at a table in an interrogation room. One of the detectives came out to get coffee, saw me and said, "Watch him."

I looked at Sammy from the doorway for a few seconds. He sat handcuffed to a metal chair bolted to the floor.

I asked him if he lived on 17th Street, and he said, "Yeah."

I noticed he wore a necklace. I got close enough to see the name *Anwar* on the necklace.

"That your name?" I asked, pointing to the necklace.

"Yeah," he said. "Anwar Abdul Wizbang."

I said, I thought your name was Sammy Smith.

He said, 'That's just my slave name."

---

[30] The final task performed by a detective when processing an arrest is to enter their name in the arrest book. This is known as *booking them*. When cops say "hit the books" the meaning is: they were actually arrested and are officially in the system.

"Oh," I said.

At this point, the detective came back with a cup of coffee and said, "Thanks, kid."

I backed out, and he shut the door.

Months later, on nightwork, I heard Ed come over the air with a car stop. He was running a male to see if there were any warrants. *Running* is cop talk for having the dispatcher, *run the name through the computer database*, looking for warrants.

Out of the radio comes the name: *Anwar Abdul Wizbang.*

I immediately grabbed the receiver.

I told the dispatcher to tell 6 car to use caution with that male. Ed was on patrol car 176; the dispatcher knew what I meant. I also told them I was on the way to back him up, and that they might want to start a wagon to his location.

I rocketed to Ed's location. Ed was standing outside the front door of his car, and Sammy was standing between his car and Ed.

I went straight at Sammy.

As I passed Ed, I took his handcuffs from their case.

I smiled and said, "Hi, Sammy." as I turned him around and handcuffed him.

Ed trusted me, but he was still wondering what I was doing.

I said to Ed, "Meet Sammy Smith, AKA: Anwar Abdul Wizbang."

"Sammy happens to be wanted for homicide, Aren't you, Sammy?" I said.

Sammy slipped.

He said, "Oh, I beat that."

Half-lies never work. I could tell by the look on his face he was lying. I opened the back of Ed's car and put him in.

I told Ed to keep an eye and went to my car to get the GRM.

I asked Sammy for his real date of birth.

I said, "Run him with that date of birth and the name Sammy Smith." It took the dispatcher about 10 seconds to respond. They called directly to the wagon on its way to us.

Dispatcher, *"1701…are you enroute to 176's location?"*

1701 responded, "We're pulling up now."

The dispatcher said, "Take the prisoner directly to homicide and use caution."

The dispatcher said, "176 use caution with that prisoner; he's wanted for homicide. We have the homicide division on the phone. They want you to bring him directly to 8th and Race[31]."

Ed looked at me and said, "Thanks."

I said, "No problem, brother."

I watched the wagon crew take Sammy out of Ed's car and search him. They put him in the wagon and took off. Ed jumped in his car and zoomed after them. I resumed patrol.

That's how it's done.

---

[31] 8th and Race Streets was the location of the department's main headquarters. Some important units were also headquartered here, among them, the Homicide Division charged with the investigation of all homicides in the city. We usually referred to it as 8th and Race. Civilians called it the Round-House, because of its circular shape.

Chapter 70

The Crying Black Belt

Ed and I were working different cars. The dispatcher sent us to the same disturbance. Someone in a karate uniform was harassing folks on the 2100 block of Pierce Street. I pulled into the block at the same time as Ed.

Here was a man, about twenty-three years old, wearing a karate uniform with a black belt. He was shouting and inviting all comers to a fight.

Sitting and leaning against a car was a man with a bloody nose, nursing a black eye.

As Ed and I approached, the black belt looked at us, went into a stance and put up both fists. He let out a yell and settled back into his stance with a slow hissing sound, like a tire going flat.

He set his face to stare us down. Ed and I both studied Karate and knew what someone with a black belt could do. We looked at the man for a moment, looked at each other and simultaneously reached back and unsnapped the safety straps that secure our service revolvers in their holster.

The sudden quiet atmosphere caused the snap to appear greatly amplified. Time froze, the black belt in his Karate stance and us in our *hands on the gun-ready stance*. Everyone was waiting to see who would make the first move.

Suddenly, loud and pathetic sobs came from our Karate friend. He dropped his hands, put them behind him, and turned his back to us.

Without missing a tick, Ed moved up behind Mr. Dojo and snapped a pair of handcuffs on his wrists.

The loud sobs continued as we walked him over and placed him in the back of Ed's car to wait for the wagon.

Ed looked at me and said, "You never know. He might have known something."

This led to some knowing laughter on our part and a ride to the catchment center for our black belt.

Chapter 71

Burglars in the Kitchen

I mentioned in my previous book I believe, to some extent, Aspies are immune to PTSD, but if situations like this arose more often, I think it may have breached, or at least dented, one of my thresholds.

I hold the belief that anyone who suffers from remorse or has nightmares about what they did stems from what they did. I believe if you avoid things you'll regret, you won't suffer later from guilt or PTSD or whatever.

Having written all that, however, I did have dreams about *this* event for years afterwards.

Early evening, as it was starting to get dark, I got a call on my sector of a *burglary-in-progress, burglars-there-now.*

This is the worst burglary call you can get. It means the homeowner called 911 and told the dispatcher burglars were in their house, *now.*

I was there in less than a minute. Ed arrived to back me up. It was a typical South Philly row house with three steps leading to the front door.

A window opened on the second floor, and a woman said, "They're in the kitchen." and threw down the key to the front door. I caught the key and inserted it into the lock.

Few homes in this neighborhood are single-family houses. They are almost all duplexes, single-family row homes converted into two apartments, one on the first floor and one on the second floor.

When you open the front door, you come into a vestibule, where you find a locked door to the first-floor apartment and a stairwell leading to a locked door to the second-floor apartment.

It was common for someone to throw down a key to enter these houses because the owner or manager of this type of property invariably lived on the second floor and kept a key to the first floor. They chose to live on the second floor, so they didn't hear the stomping of feet on their ceiling from the upstairs occupants.

I expected when I opened this door, I would encounter a second locked door and would have to unlock it as well.

I turned to Ed and said, "Ready?"

"Ready," he replied.

As I turned the key, someone on the inside yanked the door out of my hand! Naturally, I expected the burglars. I thought something spooked them and they were now on their way out as we were coming in.

Instinctively, I rocked back and rotated my service revolver up in the direction of the doorway with my finger on the trigger. I was starting to apply pressure.

It takes twelve pounds of pull to fire these revolvers; I was at six pounds when I saw the face of the nine-year-old girl!

After the woman threw me the key so she could stay safely upstairs, she sent her nine-year-old daughter down to *"Open the door for the police."* This was one of the rare single-family homes on the block.

It's difficult to describe the level of emotion that was surging through my system. I was envisioning the aftermath of having shot a nine-year-old girl and still had the burglars to deal with.

Add: my thoughts for *mother-of-the-year* safe upstairs.

I told the girl, "Go back upstairs."

I could feel Ed's hand on my shoulder.

He said, "What the fuck?"

I walked through the house directly to the kitchen, where there were sounds of scurrying, and things knocked over, hitting the floor. I peeked around the corner into the kitchen to see four large rats fighting over a loaf of bread.

I said, "Fucking rats."

I holstered my gun and drew the stick. I launched at the rats and clubbed one in the head. The others began to scurry away, but Ed was on them with his stick. We smacked all four dead on the kitchen table and floor.

When we were satisfied we got them all, we walked back to the front door. The woman was at the top of the stairs.

She said, "Did you get them?"

I said, "Yes, we did. It was rats."

She said, "Rats?"

"Yes," I answered "Rats".

I added, "Don't worry, we got them all."

I looked at Ed and said, "Let's get the *f* out of here."

He said, "I'm with you, brother."

The report read: Report of Burglary in Progress, UNFOUNDED.

I dreamt for years a constant repetition of an out-of-body picture of the door pulled from my hand and the specter of the revolver's hammer moving in its rearward arc. In times like these, with danger imminent, my vision became panoramic. I could see the girl's face and the hammer moving at the same time.

It repeated over and over for months after the event and recured for years. This is one of the questionable sides of the eidetic memory that came with the syndrome.

My mind was searching for a way to resolve it, more importantly, what *could* have happened. If not for the stock double-action revolver with the factory twelve-pound trigger pull, the outcome would have been horrific.

This is why, to this day, I won't carry an automatic pistol unless it is one made to mimic the action of the revolver with at least twelve pounds of pull on the first shot.

I see many instances in the news of incidents where a weapon of this design would have prevented unintended shootings as this one had.

I get a pounding headache telling this story.

Chapter 72

Outside Agencies
Try Their Street Skills

After work one day, I went to visit my parents, who still lived in SW Philly. I grew up in a row house on a street with seventy homes. Everyone there knew everyone else. Getting away with anything required street smarts and being very sneaky; outsiders stood out like boats on the horizon.

I had parked in front of the house and was enjoying a nice visit when the phone rang.

Mom answered and said, "Michael, it's for you."

It was a neighbor. She said hello and asked, "Did some of your police friends come with you to visit your mom?"

I said, "No, why do you ask?"

She said, "Because right after you pulled up, a car parked in front of your house, and the two men sitting in it look like undercover cops."

I thanked her and went up to the second-floor front bedroom. I knew unless whoever it was *was* savvy, they would not be looking up to the second floor. I peeked through the blinds *Dans le mode de la Cherchez la femme.*[32]

---

[32] *Cherchez la femme* - Go find the woman. An expression popular among French detectives. The Philly version was, "Look for the woman with the flat nose."

I could see the Ford LTD with the two suited boobs "acrossed[33]" the street (remember, we're in SW Philly). They were on the wrong side of the street, a guaranteed visit from the sector car, and the reason the neighbor noticed them. They were craning their necks to peer in the front window of Mom's house.

The neighbor would normally call the police, but having seen me arrive, followed by what she perceived to be other cops, she called me instead. The only time anyone on my street called the police was when someone parked on the wrong side of the street, and it was almost a guarantee that if you parked there, someone would call. This was a high-level safety issue for everyone.

I heard the feebs were following off-duty rookies, but this was the first time I saw them. They followed me all the way from the 17th.

I was to learn the feds were anything but street smart; notwithstanding their reputation as crack investigators, they were like witches reaching water when they came into the neighborhoods.

While they worked on the kinks they would soon have in their necks, I slipped out the back door, walked to the corner at the far end of the driveway, and down the street behind their car.

I was at the driver's side door for at least a minute, watching them attempting to watch me.

I got bored and knocked on the driver's window. Both jumped. When they turned around and realized it was me, the driver immediately started the car. I motioned for him to roll down the window, but he was frantically trying to get the engine going and when it finally fired up, he threw it into gear, and they took off like scorched cats.

When I got to work the next day and told the story in the locker room, everyone gathered around to hear. This pissed everyone off, even

---

[33] Philly vernacular. In Philly things on the other side of the street are *acrossed* the street.

the ones who didn't like me. It was one thing to have them in the district, but following us home was too much.

We mentioned it to our sergeant.

He said, "That's nothing. They follow me home, to the store, to the cleaners and back to work almost every day."

Enough!

Now we looked for them and finally caught a team off guard and rousted them from their car. I wasn't there. The guys who told the story said they made the mistake of doing it during a disturbance when five or six cars and a wagon showed up and blocked them in.

They couldn't drive off, and the officers got them out of the car, demanded their ID and inspected their guns.

None of us saw them again, either in the district or out after that adventure. I think the experience of a bunch of twenty-something rookies pushing you around and relieving you of your gun was just a bit uncomfortable.

Chapter 73

A Lost District Car

"Just because you're paranoid doesn't mean they're not watching you."

– Bob Hurst

With the paranoia spread by the department, the bosses, other officers and the news media, I was bound to catch some of it.

Getting a steady car is a challenge. If you don't get one, you're basically an orphan. I had wrangled my way into patrol car 1711. Conscious of the precariousness of a permanent car and the atmosphere in the district, which you could cut with a knife, I was watching my Ps and Qs.

I was approaching Point Breeze and 23rd when I noticed a police car parked on my sector. You can always tell if a car belongs there because we can hear all the assignments over the radio. I suspected this car didn't belong there from a block away, and as I got closer, I knew it didn't.

It was a car from a completely different district. And not a close one. This car was from miles away in North Philly.

At first, I figured I would confront the officer and see what they were doing there, so I got out and looked for them. There were no commercial establishments on that corner, so I assumed they were in someone's house.

I got nervous. Suppose this officer was from the old 17th and came back to continue whatever behavior got them kicked out in the first place. People will see a police car and assume it's the sector cop – me.

After a few minutes, I called the dispatcher and said, *"Can you have 17-B come to my location?"*

17-B arrived in short order. Our sergeants were good that way. They didn't make a big deal over the radio; they just showed up.

He said, "What's up?"

I pointed to the car.

His face said, "WTF?"

I told him I spent a few minutes looking before I called him, but couldn't find the officer.

He immediately got on the radio and said, *"Radio, what is 234's assignment?"*

The dispatcher clicked into J-Band and said, *"South band to J-Band."* *"17-B is requesting 234's assignment."*

Then J-Band connected to East Band, and East Band replied, *"East to J, 234 is out of service at the tire shop at Front and Wolf."*

All the chatter should give you some idea of how far off his assigned sector this car was. Front and Wolf was over 2.5 miles from the location where the sergeant and I stood, and that distance off from the most direct route back to the 23rd District. In a city where a sector can be two by three blocks, this was a long way off.

The sergeant thanked the dispatcher as the officer from 234 appeared on the corner.

He went straight to his car to get in and leave, but the sergeant called out, "Officer."

234 stopped and looked at him.

The sergeant said, "Come over here."

"What is your assignment in the 17th District?"

The officer said, "I'm on my way back from the tire shop."

The sergeant said, "You're a little out of your way, aren't you?"

He couldn't help himself. He gave me the stink-eye for calling my sergeant. This was not a good move with my sergeant, especially after the incident with the burglary team.

The sergeant said, "Where did you just come from?"

The officer said, "I stopped to see a friend."

The sergeant said, "At which address?"

The officer replied with an address.

The sergeant snapped, "Get your log."

Getting religion, he complied smartly.

The sergeant noted the time, and with the red-ink-pen supervisors used to sign our logs, he wrote the address the officer gave him and signed the officer's log.

The sergeant told me to note the address and incident in my log, and he, the sergeant, made sure the officer saw him write it in the sergeant's own log.

He handed the officer's log back and said, "Get back to your own district and don't make any more detours through the 17th unless you have official business here."

The officer took his log, slunk back to his car and left.

I hated to do that, but with the situation as it was, I was content to be responsible for what I did, and I expected others to take responsibility for what they did.

The mistrust the veteran officers harbored for us rookies was rapidly becoming mutual. I certainly didn't trust any I didn't personally know.

Remember the THE MAGIC MEMO story? The sergeant got into his car and called me over.

Chapter 74

The Detective Test

My sergeant faced a situation dictated by circumstances. He wanted to be a detective sergeant, but he was in uniform supervising us. His true love was the detective bureau.

He said, "So, are you going to take the detective's test?" (Announced that day.)

I said, "No, I don't want to be a detective."

He got visibly upset. He ripped me a new one. He said that's where all the action was, and I needed to do it. It wasn't a suggestion.

I did my usual recon and found out I was competing against 9,000 police officers for 200 open spots in the detective bureau. I saw no trouble with the test itself, but I knew military veterans[34] received ten extra points, and every officer got points added for longevity[35].

Without the veteran's preference points, zero points for longevity and less than a year on the job, it would be tough to get in. I figured I would have to pull close to a perfect score on the exam to even have a shot.

That part didn't bother me.

This is not arrogance. Just the way I saw it. We don't do arrogance. We're often accused of it, but it's just unvarnished honesty.

---

[34] Military veterans received ten extra points on any test administered by the department. This program was known as *veteran's preference*.
[35] The city used a formula to add extra points to promotional exams based on the number of years you were on the job.

So, I thought about it for a while. There was a flyer in the district announcing the test; you must apply at the city personnel office; the application period was from May 1st to May 20th.

I was starting to sense something. If there was an open period....

I called city hall and asked, "If, after one takes the test, and the veteran's preference and longevity are figured in, several people have the same score, who goes first?"

They answered, "The person whose application was time-stamped first."

I asked for clarification; they replied, "You have to come to the personnel office in City Hall to apply. When you hand in your application, we timestamp every application with the same time clock."

"If you and someone else have the same score on the test and you got your application stamped at 9:00 AM on the 1st and the other person has theirs stamped at 10:00 AM on the 1st, you go first."

Now I saw the angle. At three in the morning May 1st, I boarded a trolley car to City Hall. At four in the morning, I was standing in line, waiting for the door to open to the personnel office.

I laughed; there were nine guys already there. But, when the door opened at 9:00 AM, there were 2,000 people behind me. That time clock stamped over 5,500 applications before the open application period ended.

After my promotion, I called City Hall and asked how many got the same score. I found out there were 20. I was among the 20. The three guys behind me and I made the cut. After that, they threw out the test as expired.

I had read *the book*[36] and understood gamesmanship. If not, I would have lazily applied for the test and missed promotion.

Out of 5,500 persons who took the test, after calculations, I ranked 183.

Historically, they promote 200 in the first wave, but due to cutbacks, affirmative action, and who knows what else, it took them almost two years to get to 183. After that, the list was over two years old, and a new test mandated.

I had synthesized *Gamesmanship* to a new level.

---

[36] *The Theory and Practice of GAMESMANSHIP* by Stephen Potter. I get into more detail about gamesmanship in my first book: *ASPERGERS. WHAT'S YOUR EXCUSE?*

Chapter 75

Botched Assassination

On my first trip to internal affairs, for God knows what, the staff inspector[37] perused my file and said, "Kid, you've kicked up a lot of dust in a year." A sniper with a similar notion was about to kick up some of his own.

I got it; I was active. A favorite saying of one of the instructors in the academy came to mind:

"You can't get in trouble if you don't do anything."

I met folks in diametrically opposed camps who utilized this saying. Some to dissuade activity and thereby trouble (in their minds a good thing), and others mocking those who never got in trouble, insinuating they never got in trouble simply because they never did anything (in their minds a bad thing).

I think the staff inspector was surprised by the *amount* of activity. He didn't seem all that interested either way. He just wanted a story to tell so he could close his investigation. He got it, and everyone left happy.

There were bosses who wanted you to *aggressively patrol* and others who wanted you to *sit on your hands*. Regardless of what you did, somebody was going to be disappointed.

The bad guys were all in favor of you sitting on your hands. When you didn't, they got upset. So, given the amount of activity that got me sent to IA and the remarks of someone who does nothing but investigate cops, it's no surprise some bad guys were not pleased with me.

---

[37] Staff inspector was a rank between captain and inspector - they worked only in Internal Affairs (IA).

I maintained a certain routine. Routine is important to people with Aspergers but can be a problem for a police officer. It was a small routine, but a routine nonetheless. When I got out of roll call, I would always service my car.

I would check for damage, leaks, oil, and the function of the lights and siren. I would pull over into the driveway behind headquarters and fill it with gas. I wanted to make sure if I ever got into *hot pursuit* of a car bound for New Jersey, I could make it all the way to the ocean.

So, on any day, you could find me at the gas pump within the first ten minutes of any shift.

We were working night work. I had been in court that morning. When you have court in the morning on a day when you're scheduled to work nightwork, you could elect to come in two hours late and work six in the evening to midnight as your full eight-hour shift.

My sergeant, from across the street at least, resembled me in general appearance. We were the same race, height, weight and build.

On this night his car was in the shop and he was using my car, 1711.

Now, one might not be able to make out a face from the distance from the mouth of the alley where the shooter stood to the gas pumps where my sergeant stood, but you can clearly identify a thin white guy who is 6 feet tall, wearing a police uniform.

It's especially easy if he's driving a patrol car with 1711 in large reflective numbers visible on the top, back and sides.

The prevailing theory is the man in the alley was there for *me*, and since I was in court and the sergeant was using my car, I was about to catch a break because he was waiting for me with a .30-06 pump action hunting rifle. A gun and caliber combination which, equipped as it was with a 3x9 variable scope, could kill a bear at 500 yards.

The assassin was 30 yards away.

He fired two shots at the sergeant. The sergeant dove for cover when the first round exploded a foot over his head, turning twelve inches of concrete wall into a cloud of dust!

The second round went, literally high and to the right, penetrating the mesh-reinforced window to the cell room, where it exploded against the steel and porcelain, wounding a prisoner with shrapnel.

The sergeant prepared to return fire but could not acquire the shooter because, after the second shot, he dropped the rifle and retreated down the alley. The alley led behind homes on several streets, into any of which he could have escaped.

When I came to work at 6:00 PM, the place was in an uproar.

The crime lab was there processing the scene, detectives were there holding the rifle, and the squad was ogling the modifications to the wall and window: the scar of a foot-long chunk of concrete, vaporized by the first shot and the clean hole in the steel wire reinforced window made by the second.

When I showed up, everyone stopped what they were doing and stared.

Leaving me to wonder, "What have I done now?"

The story was related to me with the caution, "He was probably after you."

I thought, *maybe,* but the sergeant was not the most popular person in the neighborhood either. It made sense the regular operator of the car was the likely target, but I thought the sergeant did wear glasses and a different hat.

Maybe he *was* trying to shoot me. I checked in, got my car and never gave it a second thought.

I did look over my shoulder a little more, but nothing much changed as far as I was concerned. When you work in Dodge City, people tend to shoot at you. This was not the first time – it wouldn't be the last.

Chapter 76

Mobile Handgun Collection

When you show an interest in guns within the police department, you immediately get a reputation with some folks as a *gun nut*. I used the term in front of a psychiatrist on one occasion – he cringed.

I saw myself more as a *gun aficionado* or, during my more English moments, a *gun fancier*.

In the 1970s, guns were anathemata within the City. Few people carried them, and those who did got sideways looks. This paradigm permeated the Philly psyche to the point even police officers got the attitude *any* guns were bad, including those carried by other officers.

The gun issued by the department was something they were stuck with and which many carried only on duty. Some condescended to purchase a compact *off-duty gun* for their own personal protection, but in my experience, most leaned to the left of center on the subject.

In one of several run-ins with bosses concerning the subject of *guns*, I heard a staff inspector say, "I wouldn't carry a gun off duty. When I came on (sometime in the 1950s, I would guess by his age), the department *required* us to carry off duty, and I refused."

I would consider him on the West end of the continuum.

Tony was on the other.

Tony was the army expert shooter I met in the academy. Remember the *Come to Jesus* event over who was the better shot?

I ran into Tony one night in the lounge. It was warm outside and even warmer inside, so I was surprised to find him supervising the dance floor wearing an army field jacket.

I inquired.

He opened the coat slightly, and I could see the .44 magnum revolver in the shoulder holster. I looked further and found the service revolver stuck in his waistband, a .45 automatic in a small-of-the-back-holster and a 2-inch - .38 Special snubby on his ankle.

He was closer to the right end of the continuum, and the expression *gun-nut* would float through my head after this incident, but only briefly. He was either carrying every gun he owned, or he owned many more guns than I.

My take was more on the idea the gun was like the sword of the Samurai. It was a badge of office, much like that of an officer in the military. It was a show of force, a kind of sword-rattling prop. And, most importantly it was the last line of defense when all other measures failed.

Along with the sharpening of the proficiency in the gun's use, should that ever become necessary, shooting was also a hobby and embodied the qualities of accuracy, precision and proficiency. I enjoyed these qualities.

I liked to be good at something I liked, and I also liked to be good at something required. The job required a gun on duty. If I ever needed to use it, I wanted to be as good at it as I possibly could. I didn't want to miss something I meant to shoot or, God forbid, hit something I didn't mean to shoot.

So, I explored different types of guns, and I practiced. This got me labeled by some as a gun nut.

Oddly enough, when promoted to detective, and the squad discovered I could touch type, a skill even more rare in the police department, no one called me a *typewriter-nut*.

The captain even made it a point to hang one of my first reports up as an example of what a report should look like, but no one ever called me a *report nut*.

They called me a brownie, but that's another story.

The bottom line is the gun was the ultimate trump card. If the time came to use it in an irreversible situation of deadly force, there was no time to rethink, *I should have practiced more.*

To me, it was as a fighter plane was to a military pilot, the sword was to the Samurai, or the typewriter was to the detective or now as a writer.

Stand by for a view from another angle.

Chapter 77

A 5" that Didn't Work

"And now for something completely different."

— Monty Python

Here's a glimpse at the opposite end of the continuum. As I mentioned earlier, all the officers in the new 17th District were rookies straight from the academy. Supervisors were not. Naturally, anyone above the rank of Police Officer was a veteran officer, so our supervisors were veterans, screened and found suitable to stay.

A Corporal in his fifties supervised the operations room. At the time *he* went through the academy, each officer provided his own gun, so whereas the rookies carried the exact same gun issued by the city, he carried a relic of the 1950s.

It was a five-inch barreled version of the gun we carried with the older-style tapered barrel.

There is cop talk for all this. We carried a *four-inch*. Cop talk for a gun with a four-inch barrel. The corporal's relic was a *five-inch*, so the chapter title is grammatically correct for those of you who might be worried.

The corporal's gun was a literal *blast from the past*. It *looked* old. (It was also Ugly with a capital "U", but we won't get into that.) His holster would have been state-of-the-art in the Wild West.

Our guns were the most recent issue; they wore larger, smarter grips, the latest magnum-style barrel and were *brand* new. And, our leather, such as it was, was also brand new.

One fine day, we all packed up and went to the range for some plinking. Plinking is what the academy staff called informal practice shooting at the range. We took the corporal with us.

At the command to commence firing, the corporal got off one shot, and his revolver failed.

The instructor took him into the range gun shop so the gunsmiths could look at his revolver. Here's what they found:

The revolver, covered in a nice patina of rust, sat in the corporal's holster for at least the last ten years. Today was the first time it ten years it saw daylight.

When the gunsmiths prized it open, they found ammunition with green oxidation on the brass. When brass with nickel plating has green oxidation, it's been rusting for a looooong time.

The gunsmiths could not get the gun to cycle; they couldn't get the hammer and trigger to work and, therefore, couldn't get the cylinder to revolve, so they disassembled it.

Inside the lock works (the inside mechanism), they found some kind of gunk that froze the parts so nothing could move.

They asked the corporal what he used to lubricate the gun, and he said, "Machine oil."

The gunsmiths cringed.

Guns require a special lubricating oil that resists hardening.

The corporal was injecting this non-gun oil into his revolver on a regular basis, and it hardened, freezing the internal parts. The gun required complete disassembly, deep cleaning with a special solvent, drying, proper lubrication and reassembly.

The corporal returned to the firing line with a functional revolver.

This is an extreme and real example, but obviously not an impossible scenario.

Imagine if he needed the gun to save his life.

If the first shot didn't do the job, and we would have to factor in even if it did go off, the ammo was so old it probably would have just made it out of the barrel, he would have been in a bad way.

Herc's take was, "I think he stores his gun in the toilet tank."

I'd rather be the gun nut for practicing and taking care of my equipment.

Chapter 78

The Never-ending Gun Argument

"You know as well as I, most shootings are with a .22."

- Ed

I've been watching the heated exchange about guns now for 50 years, but the simple fact remains that, as Wild Bill Hickock said, "It's all about accuracy."

You could walk from New York to France on the studies conducted during *my* lifetime, resulting in "innovations" in gun and bullet designs every year. Studies and design improvements by folks who have been using the same toothbrush design the entire time, yet the arguments continue to rage.

The argument centers on something called *stopping power*. This is euphemism for *killing power* because *that* would be tacky. The argument for the euphemism is that we want to *stop* fights, explaining many people have gone on to kill other people after suffering mortal wounds, so the ideal is to *stop* the actor's actions vs *kill* the actor.

Stop, kill, tomāto, tomăto

It would be cumbersome to go into detail with these reports, so I'll boil them down:

Bigger is better. Seems intuitive until someone substitutes faster for bigger, then better-designed better than either, and the whole thing starts again.

The caliber of a gun is based on the diameter of the bullets in the gun's cartridges. For example, a .45 has a .45-inch bullet diameter.

Remember, *Bigger is better?*

The army went from the .45 to a .38 because it was a better design but switched back to the .45 because the .38 wasn't *stopping* the bad guys.

Now, they're back to .38, actually a 9mm which is a ruse, because 9mm is simply German for .38.

The FBI did something similar: .45 to .38 to 9mm. In between, they experimented with the .357 Magnum, which is a pumped-up .38, but decided it was *too* powerful.

Then they got all shot up by bad guys because the FBI's *nines* were not powerful enough against the bad guy's assault rifles. (a whole 'nother animal)

So, they upped it to 10mm but quickly decided *that* was too powerful and adopted the .40 caliber, which, if you do the math, is 10mm. Now they're back to the nines.

If anyone discovers a pattern, hit the contact button on my website.

Something else besides stopping power is at work here, but none of it matters if you can't hit what you're shooting at.

One of the world *experts* on the subject was the late Colonel Bill Cooper, a promoter of the .45, reinforcing his position, saying, *"The smallest gun I'll carry is a .380 Automatic. But again, I don't drive on bald tires either."*

He said this to discourage folks from carrying .25s and .32s, also popular at the time.

The .380 although the same diameter bullet, is weaker than the .38 Special, the standard for police at the time. You know, the one the army replaced with the .45.

Again, it seems Wild Bill was on to something about accuracy as the primary issue.

Let's reduce it to the absurd, *Reductio ad absurdum.*

Assume the .45 is at the top of the heap, being the biggest. (Bear with me here.)

John Browning, who designed the .45 and every other gun on the planet, decided to design a .25, which looks like a miniature .45.

- The .45 shoots a 230-grain bullet at 835 feet per second, producing *356*-foot pounds of energy.

- The .25 shoots a 50-grain bullet at 760 feet per second, producing *64*-foot pounds of energy.

The .45 is *5.5* times bigger in size *and* power than the .25.

The first homicide I responded to in the 17th was our man in the Cabaret with the 9mm. You remember Sunny and his *nine*. I was basically an onlooker at that shooting.

The first time the dispatcher assigned the paperwork to me was in a local bar not too far from there. This is how responsibility is determined for an assignment. Someone is *assigned the paperwork*. That means they are responsible for the *incident report* (the first *official* police report), recorded on a form that all officers carry.

Here's the scene:

The front door was open. I carefully peeked inside. The bartender said, "Come in, he's gone."

When I entered, there were a half dozen patrons in the bar, the victim was lying on his back on the floor.

The victim had been sitting on a bar stool when a man walked in the front door and confronted him. The man on the stool stood and faced him. The bad guy fired one shot from a .25 automatic pistol, which entered the victim's heart.

He dropped dead on the spot.

A funny aside: the empty shell ejected from the automatic pistol and plopped into the drink of the man who was sitting next to the shooting victim. When I approached him, he was frozen, staring at the empty casing in the glass as if he thought it was going to explode. I picked up the glass and moved it so he could relax enough to tell me what happened.

A man with a gun not much bigger than a fig bar just terrorized the bar and everyone in it. He did it with a gun small enough to hide in a pack of cigarettes.

Apparently, they weren't *too* terrorized because they resumed drinking. Or, the shooting *precipitated* their drinking, I don't know.

Anyway, one shot from a .25 auto = one stone-cold dead adult male.

On another evening, a month or so later, the dispatcher sent me to the scene of a shooting on a nearby corner. An argument between two men went bad, and one produced a .45 auto pistol and shot at the other. The victim was standing next to a stop sign. The first shot went high, blew a half-inch hole in the stop sign and kept on going.

The victim turned to run.

The man with the gun aimed a bit more carefully, and the second shot hit the victim square in the spine at heart level.

The victim was wearing a denim jacket. The bullet, a hollow point, one of the most recent *improvements* at the time meant to make the .45 an even *better man-stopper*, drilled into the man's back a short distance, bounced off and fell to the ground.

I recovered the bullet. The hollow point was stuffed with human tissue and denim fibers. Don't read into this – denim is *not* bulletproof!

The victim fell but recovered enough to sit up on the curb. He walked to the ambulance when it arrived and climbed into the back for the trip to the hospital.

Aside from a new dimple in his back or *back belly button*, he suffered no other obvious damage.

Remember the .380 Col. Jeff compared to new tires? Just up the street from the bar where the man killed the patron with the .25, a robbery was committed by a bad guy with a .380.

He decided it would be a good idea to shoot at the responding officer, who ducked behind his car. The .380 punched right through the metal of the police car.

Thank God the officer was unharmed.

But, my respect for the .380 faded when a shooting occurred in a bar where someone fired three shots into a bouncer's midsection from three inches away.

The bouncer was particularly corpulent, so the bullets didn't even penetrate the fat. The fat stopped them, and they never made it to his vitals. The doctor was able to pull them out with a pair of hemostats.

So, what's the point?

The point is to practice, focus on accuracy and be sure to hit what you're shooting at. If you're not confident you can safely do that, keep it, whatever it is, in the holster.

Chapter 79

Dickter Kopf

Another of Col. Cooper's lessons was never to carry an untested gun. I was about to learn this one the hard way.

We didn't have school buses to take us to school when I was growing up. We rode on Philadelphia Transportation Company or PTC busses, trains and trolley cars.

I walked to grammar school because it was only a block from my house. A requirement, my mother told me, when she chose the house the year I was born. She wanted the school within easy walking distance, so we could come home for lunch.

High school, however, was a different story. We lived 2.9 miles away from the school, and it took about 45 minutes to an hour to get there. We took a trolley car from 65th Street to 49th and a bus from 49th Street to Chestnut Street.

There was a large and notorious public high school a block from our high school. Some of the kids who attended that school would ride on the bus on 49th Street.

One spring day, I sat down next to one of these kids. I noticed a tattoo on his left arm that read: *Aires*.

I took an interest, because I'm an Aires. I looked over and caught his eye.

I said, "Are you an Aires?"

He said, "Yes, why?"

There wasn't a whole lot of instant trust in this neighborhood. But I would talk to anyone. I learned this from Mom, watching her talk to everyone. (I didn't yet know the wisdom of *Min-yer-own-biness*. I still don't have the wiring for it.)

I said, "I was born in March, so I was wondering."

He brightened up a little and said he was born in April. We were been born eight days apart.

We held a conversation during the rest of the ride, talking about school, sports and girls. I saw him often during the commute and can still see his face. He was mixed race, light-skinned, with light brown hair and unusual blue eyes. Not someone most people would easily forget, let alone me.

I learned during these rides his name was Dickter Kopf. Seemed like a nice fellow.

Fast forward to Spring 1978, Roll call in the 17th:

"Remember to keep up with your quips[38] and pick up today's hot sheet. Also, Homicide sent over a wanted sheet for a homicide suspect. Pick those up on the table."

As I waited to get my hot sheet and the BOLO, I could hear the officers in front of me making remarks.

"Man, he's cute." came the sarcastic remark from one.

"Yeah, that's a face you won't forget." said another.

I ignored this crap as usual until I got to the table.

There was Dickter.

---

[38] Quips was an informal term for GRMs - little *cop-commercials* radio broadcast during the tour. Other departments call them BOLOs - Be On the Lookout.

Wanted for homicide in the 18th District, Dickter Kopf. Last seen in the area of 45th and Springfield. Caution: Armed with a Gun. I read further into the description, it described Dickter as Black with blue eyes, light brown hair and a tattoo that read *Aires*.

Now I knew what happened to Dickter.

Several times during that shift, the radio dispatcher quipped, *Wanted for Homicide in the 18th District. Dickter Kopf. Black male, blue eyes, Aires Tattoo on the left arm. Caution: armed with a gun.* (*Quip* was cop talk for these little reminders the dispatcher repeated every so often.)

This repeated for that week and into the next.

I could see Dickter's face each time I heard it.

During that week, I dropped into the local gun store to pick up an off-duty gun that was somewhat easier to carry than the large one I was currently carrying. It was compact and sexy. A must-have item.

I also bought a box of ammunition. It was a new design, and although I thought the hollow point configuration of the bullets looked a little too blunt for the intended purpose, the gun store assured me it was good stuff.

I knew better, but I couldn't wait to carry that pistol. I knew from reading Col. Cooper's training book not to carry any handgun, especially an automatic pistol, before thoroughly testing it with the ammunition you intend to carry. The Col. suggested he would never carry any pistol until he personally fired 200 rounds of the ammo through with 100% reliability.

But, being young and impatient, I loaded it up, stuck it in my holster and started off for work.

I was driving on Springfield Avenue, a street cut diagonally through West Philly to the U of P campus. It was close to the route I used to take to high school.

It was early spring, at about three in the afternoon.

1977 into 1978 was a particularly harsh winter with lots of snow. There were still piles of it in the street. I could see someone coming toward me, walking in the street. He was avoiding the piles of snow on the side of the street assembled there by plows.

I slowed, I couldn't cross the white line yet to move over to let him pass. I stopped, watching him approach. He was wearing a leather jacket and jeans and was leading two Doberman Pinschers.

Something about him was familiar.

As he got closer, the traffic coming in the other direction passed by, and I was able to pull forward by crossing the white line, giving both of us room to navigate. At this point, he was right off my right bumper.

I looked at him.

He looked at me.

It was Dickter.

I hesitated for a second, and my car began to roll slowly forward. He was next to my passenger window now. For a split second, we made eye contact.

A million thoughts raced through my mind.

What should I do? Should I do anything? What would be the smart thing to do?

Should I simply stop and say, "Hi, Dickter, remember me?"

What if I got out and confronted him?

He was sure to let the dogs loose. And what about this untested pistol? What if it doesn't work?

What to do?!

I could try to bluff someone who was obviously ridiculously street-wise, was enormously wary and guarded (Why else the dogs?), and was also known to carry a gun (Wouldn't you?), and hope that a police badge intimidated him enough to surrender. (Not likely.)

Or, I could be prudent.

I could note where I saw him. Look for a pay phone, and flood the area with police.

I decided to be prudent.

I drove around him. As I passed, I could see his eyes scan the car's interior. I watched in the mirror; he looked over his shoulder, a telling move.

I drove to the corner and turned into the gas station to look for a phone.

Bonanza!

There was a police car sitting in the gas station. 18 DC, the 18th district lieutenant.

I pulled my car behind his, got out, identified myself and told him who I saw. He reached for his clipboard.

He held up a photo of Dickter and said, "Him.?"

"Yes, I just saw him."

"Get in."

I jumped into his car, and we raced to where I saw Dickter. The lieutenant notified the dispatcher. We were now back in the same spot where, less than a few minutes before, I was exchanging glances with Dickter.

No one was there.

We worked a grid, going from block to block, Nothing. Police cars flooded the area. We did this for a good fifteen minutes with no result.

Damn! I thought.

The lieutenant and I chatted for a few minutes, and I told him I was due in at 4:00 PM, so he told me to get on my way. He drove me back to my car and I started off for the 17th.

When I walked in the back door of the 17th, past the window to the operations room, the corporal called out.

He said, "Don't even change. Take your personal car and go straight to Homicide."

Off I went.

A team of Homicide Detectives were waiting.

"Are you Cubbage?" they asked.

I introduced myself; there was no chitchat. These guys were strictly business. A different class of detective.

For the entire shift, we went over my experience with Dickter. Apparently, the Lieutenant from the 18th called them about what happened; they wanted to debrief me.

I told them about seeing Dickter and how I thought it would have been a mistake to confront him. They affirmed my decision.

"He's a bad one, he is." one of the detectives said. "Shot three people in a house down on 43rd street, killed two of them."

"He's always armed." said another.

The third one nodded in agreement.

They asked me if I was sure it was him, and I told them about knowing him from high school.

Startled, one said, "You went to West Philly?!" (The notorious public high school).

I explained about the bus, and they nodded knowingly.

We went over every detail of what happened that day and every detail of my experiences with Dickter on the bus to school. Who was he with? What did you talk about? What was he wearing, and how did he behave? Was he a member of a gang, and did he have a girlfriend?

They wanted him badly. I returned the next two days to go over my story again and look at some pictures of known associates of Dickter to see if any of them were also on the bus.

The only one I recognized was Dickter.

Now, the next part has always puzzled me.

About a week after I gave the detectives all the information about Dickter and went back to my normal patrol duty, I got a call from the detectives. They said they investigated further and were unsuccessful in finding Dickter in any of the known addresses near where I saw him.

I didn't find this odd because he didn't want them to find him. It didn't surprise me I saw him because that's the area he was coming from when I would see him on the bus, so he grew up there and had roots in the neighborhood.

What also didn't surprise me was they said their investigation led them to Yeadon, Pennsylvania, where they caught up with the guy I saw.

They said he wasn't Dickter Kopf.

I said, "Then you caught up with someone else because the guy I saw the other day was Dickter Kopf."

I said Yeadon made sense because there was a constant exchange and movement between West Philly and Yeadon, and it was a good place to lie low when the police were looking for you. I grew up two blocks from Yeadon and knew the area.

The detective reiterated they followed up and located the guy I saw, but he wasn't Dickter.

I told him again I knew Dickter personally, and the guy I saw *was indeed* Dickter Kopf.

I pointed out I could see he also recognized me and we both gave thought to stopping and talking to each other, but my hesitation caused him to be wary, or he would have stopped and talked.

The detective insisted it wasn't Dickter, and I saw no reason to continue to insist and get him annoyed, so I said thanks and told him to reach out if he needed anything else. He thanked me and said goodbye.

Remember the new pistol I was carrying? I still hadn't test-fired it. I liked the feel of it and wanted to continue to carry it, so I took it to the academy on my day off to test fire.

It still held the ammunition I was carrying the day I saw Dickter and considered confronting him and the Dobermans.

I took it to the firing line, drew it and fired the first shot.

It jammed! Big time!

This type of jam is dangerous, it's called a stove pipe jam.

It jams not only the gun itself but the magazine holding the cartridges. It takes four or five movements, if you know what you're doing, to clear the damn jam.

While I was doing all this, Dickter would have been shooting me full of holes while the Dobermans ate me.

Never again would I carry any weapon before thoroughly testing it.

I never did find out what happened to Dickter, maybe in the next life.

Chapter 80

Through and Through with a .22

"'You can't make this stuff up.', doesn't quite do it here."

— The Author

A bright red circle of blood was rapidly growing around the hole in the white t-shirt just under his left collarbone. This was the scene greeting me as I stepped through the front door of the address for the call: *hospital case gunshot.*

The owner of the shirt looked me up and down and said, "What do you want?"

I said, "Well, given the bullet hole in your chest, to take you to the hospital."

I reached out and turned him around. I could see a similar hole in the back of the shirt, where the bullet exited his back. I could see the mark on the wall about 20 feet behind him where the bullet hit after passing through him.

He looked at the hole and said, "Oh, that. That's nothing."

"What happened?"

"I was with a whore earlier tonight, and I didn't pay her. Her pimp came over here, and when I answered the door, he shot me."

"Didn't you call?"

"No" he answered,

I could see a woman hovering behind him in the kitchen. I looked at her, and she nodded, indicating she was the caller, but she wouldn't come any closer.

I said, "Well, I'm here, so I have to take you to the hospital."

He walked toward the front door, and when I stepped through, he slammed the door behind me.

I knocked, and he answered. I said, "I have to take you to the hospital."

He said, "No, I don't want to go to the hospital," and shut the door again.

At about this point, the rest of the gang arrived, and the sergeant ran up and said, "What do you have?"

I said, "The guy answered the door with a bullet wound in his chest and said he didn't want to go. He slammed the door in my face."

"Don't you know he has to go to the hospital?"

"Yes, I know, but apparently, *he* doesn't. The only way to get him to go is to force him."

The sergeant called to a wagon crew and said, "Come with me."

The three of them walked to the front door, and the sergeant knocked. When the man came to the door, they pulled him out to the wagon and sped off to the hospital.

I went into the house to see if the woman was alright. She came out to meet me when they took her husband away. She said she was upstairs and heard the shot. She called 911. She didn't want to come too close to the front door in case the man came back who shot him.

I told her he would be OK in the hospital and they would call her when she could go to see him.

I looked down while I was talking to her and noticed a .22 caliber bullet on the floor. This was apparently the one that drilled the hole in her man.

I put it in my pocket. Homicide Division might catch the pimp, and having the bullet assured me some court time. Read that, overtime.

Chapter 81

A Brief Examination.

The department looks for unique individuals to work in the Juvenile Aid Division. I remembered hearing this in the academy. They said many officers found it difficult to deal with crimes involving children to the point where they couldn't be objective. I didn't like crimes against children either, but I also found crimes against women, old people, and everyone else equally distasteful. I would have dismissed this until Lou and I met the guy in his underwear.

Lou was the nicest guy in the academy. The guy everyone likes. They also liked to play tricks on him, like handcuffing him to his chair right before lunch on the day they issued us handcuffs.

I remember hearing Lou say one day, "I would take a bullet for a good job." We called our assignments *jobs*.

He was that kind of guy. He would put himself between good guy and bad guy for almost anyone. When we hit the street, he was the poster child for objectivity and restraint. And then....

I got the call. *1234 Bouvier Street (which the dispatcher pronounced Bow-veer). Abandoned Children.*

It took a second for my brain to translate the street name to Bouvier.

It was 2:00 AM.

I arrived to find two children aged five and six sitting on the front steps of a row house. Lou arrived as backup. I was talking to the children when I noticed Lou's face.

Gone was the usual fatherly, calming expression. His face stretched in an angry beet-red grimace.

One of the children was explaining to me their mom's boyfriend was over and they, the mom and boyfriend, put them out of the house for a while. They indicated this was a normal and common experience for them, and they didn't seem particularly put out by the whole affair.

Before I could do anything else, Lou startled me by pounding on the front door. Momentarily, the window on the second floor above the door opened, and a bare-chested man leaned out and said, "What do you want?"

Lou called up, "Come down here and let these children in the house!"

The man said, "We'll be down when we're finished."

Lou was now banging and kicking at the front door. I thought he was going to kick it off the hinges.

I called up, "You better come down and let them in."

About ten seconds later, the door opened. It was the man.

He started to say, "Listen here…"

That's all he got out before Lou was on him. He pushed him back into the house and up against the wall of the living room, *frisking* him.

I looked at Lou and said, "What are you doing?"

He shouted, "Frisking him."

I said, "Lou, he's in his underwear."

The only thing the guy was wearing was a pair of *briefs*.

Lou didn't care. He spun the guy around and started to give him a lecture. While this was going on, the children slid past and ran upstairs to bed.

Lou pushed the guy back against the wall and told him if he had to come back to this house because he was mistreating these children, he would haul him off to jail.

"Haul him off to jail." Catchy phrase, I thought.

At this point, what we euphemistically referred to as *mother-of-the-year* appeared on the stairwell. Now it was her turn for the Lecture.

Lou started with, "You should be ashamed of yourself", and progressed rapidly to the ever-popular, "If I have to come back…."

So, I saw it for myself. When children were involved, something happened to some officers. The guy, who was the most gentle person I knew, shed the sheep's clothing and showed his teeth.

Chapter 82

Things Happen Fast.

As I passed the side street, the shot rang out to my right. I felt the air move as the bullet *buzzed* an inch from my nose.

With my windows down, the bullet flew through the driver's compartment, entering the front passenger's window on its way to exit the driver's side. By the time I reacted, it had hit the brick wall of the house to my left. I threw the car in park and rolled out the door, gun in hand.

There was an old-timer on the corner pointing in the direction of a man running north on Dorrance Street. I took chase, but when I reached the next corner, where he turned only a few seconds ago, the neighborhood had already swallowed him. (A fleeting felon who *would* escape.)

When I returned to the older gentleman, he told me the young man pulled a gun and demanded his money. The old man was facing the street on which I was driving, and the robber was facing him with his back to me.

When the old man saw the police car, he bugged. When the robber saw *him* bug, he turned and, in one motion, as the police car pulled even with where they stood, fired a shot over his left shoulder, then fled up Dorrance Street.

I pondered what would have happened if I had seen the man before he fired the shot. I probably would have ducked. If I had ducked, my head would have been in the bullet's direct path, and instead of feeling the air displaced in front of my nose and the buzz as it passed....

"There are no atheists in foxholes."

– *William Thomas Cummings*

Chapter 83

Barry's Assist

When Barry told me in the academy that we would work together, I was skeptical. It's not that I didn't believe him; I just couldn't picture how he could arrange it. Yet here we were, standing roll call with Barry to my right nudging me in the arm.

When he first mentioned the idea I thought, *"He would have to get us assigned to the same district, in the same squad, and convince a sergeant to let two rookies work together."*

I assumed he was working on a long-range plan we could get together sometime in the future and work in a special unit.

Now he was poking me and beaming. He had pulled it off.

We worked on that wagon together for months with zero problems. There was a rule that all two-man vehicles be salt and pepper. That is, staffed by a black and a white officer.

We were the perfect team. Each time one of us was about to step on his poncho, the other would step in and hold him back. If I couldn't figure something out, he could and vice versa.

He was a big man, too. He played football for Cheyney State University, and his build told the story. He was like a tank. Samson with the wisdom of Solomon.

One evening, the dispatcher sent us to a disturbance house. I kept trying to calm the man of the house, and when he refused, I started pulling on a pair of black leather gloves, making a dramatic, clearly understood gesture.

The man said, "Oh, I know what you're doing."

He looked at Barry. Barry nodded knowingly. This pantomime worked almost every time, so we avoided most situations that might have turned violent.

Another skit we did was for me to walk in by myself. The crowd would look at me and sometimes jeer. I was never particularly physically intimidating. Most people didn't even believe I was a real cop.

Then Barry would walk up behind me.

I loved watching the people's eyes move from eye level with me up to Barry's eye level. For some reason, their smiles and laughs would disappear and remarks such as, "Oh, my God." would hasten a state of tranquility. From the men due to his size and the women for his good looks.

The first time he saved both our lives came when we were driving to our first assist officer call as a team. It was my turn to drive, and I hit the gas as Barry threw on the lights and siren.

This was not long after we all hit the 17th, so many were still unfamiliar with the streets. I was familiar because I grew up not far away and spent time in South Philly.

As I was approaching an intersection, Barry turned the siren off. I looked over at him, puzzled.

He said, "Do me a favor. Come to a full stop at the stop sign."

I shrugged and said, "OK."

As I stopped at the three-way stop (we were on a one-way street approaching a two-way street), two other police cars, both headed to the assist, blew their respective stop signs at 50 MPH.

We were going in the right direction, *they* were going in the wrong direction and in opposite directions of each other.

If not for Barry, we would all be toast!

Chapter 84

Faster than a
Speeding German Shepherd

I would never have believed that, if I had not seen it myself.

- Everybody Ever

Another thing that amazed me was Barry's incredible speed. As big and muscular as he was, he was lightning fast. The first demonstration of this was during a call to a *burglary in progress at the rear of a row of homes.*

Accessing the rear in most of the homes on our sector required coming in from either end of the block-long alley behind the houses.

The alley was a few inches over shoulder width between wooden fences that sit at the back of each home's yard. When you entered these alleys, all the dogs barked, most of them were outside dogs, alarm systems. They spent most of their lives in these yards, which resulted in the call *barking dog* earning a different meaning in the 17th than most other places.

We were several houses in from the street approaching the address of the call when we passed a yard with a German Shepard in residence. Barry was in front of me, and when he passed this yard, the German Shepherd leapt to the top of the fence, reached over, and snatched Barry's hat right off his head!

I never saw anything like this. It never occurred to me that a dog could jump that high. The fence was six feet tall.

Before I could even process it, in one blinding movement, Barry retrieved the blackjack from its recessed rear pocket, smacked the dog on the side of the head, and retrieved his hat.

Dumbfounded, I stood pondering this as he dusted off the hat, muttering, "Mutha fucka," as he put it back on his head.

I truly would not have believed that if I wasn't there.

I was to see it repeat itself several more times before the year was out.

Chapter 85

Stay Out of My Nova.

My first personal car was a 1968 Plymouth Fury painted pea green, lots of miles. When a tire would go bad, I'd go to the place where J.C. Penny's threw their old tires out and get one with enough rubber left to hold air and throw it on; always four mismatched tires, and I never balanced them. They bounced off the road at highway speeds like basketballs.

When that car died, I got a 1969 Chevy Impala with a front seat that looked like tigers claw-fought on it. I bought a front seat out of a wrecked Caprice and threw it in there. It looked nice. The manual transmission linkage would freeze when it snowed. I kept a stick to smack it so I could shift gears.

I drove the Impala until about four weeks into the academy, but I was concerned it would break down, and I wouldn't be able to make it to work. The academy was not readily accessible by public transportation, so I needed a reliable car.

I did tons of research about new cars. AS research is the kind that gets people to different planets.

I decided on a 1977 Chevy Nova. The only option I wanted was automatic transmission. I was sick of shifting gears. I was proud of my Nova. I researched the best car, made a great deal and was finally driving something new and reliable.

Now, understand a sky-blue Nova with a white top was not in vogue with the manly crowd at that time, but none of that meant anything to me. I got what I wanted, and if it wasn't pink, I didn't care what color it was.

My only issue with the car was: the driver's side door lock didn't work reliably when locked from the inside. I could lock it with the key from the outside, but if a passenger got out, pushed the button down and shut the door, it was hit or miss as to whether it locked.

One night, the Earps went to Nick's Roast Beef after nightwork. I had driven Herc and afterwards dropped him back off at headquarters to pick up his car. He got out, pushed the door lock down and shut the door. I didn't give it a second thought.

I drove through the U of P campus on my way home and stopped at a red light at 36th and Walnut. I could see the guy walk up behind the car.

At the time, I was carrying my newest acquisition, a 9mm pistol. When my man approached the Nova from the rear on Walnut Street, the nine made its way into my right hand – cocked and locked.

He came to the passenger's side and pulled the handle. The button, which Herc pushed down, popped up, enabling the dude to open the door.

As he did, he shouted over his shoulder, "I got one!"

He turned and started head-first into the car, where he was staring straight down the 9mm hole in the barrel of the pistol.

He screamed, "He's got a gun!" and his feet, which were already running down Walnut Street, dragged his legs, body and head from the car.

I could see him dive between parked cars on the side of the street, well behind my car.

He was rude. He should have asked.

I never did get that lock fixed.

Chapter 86

Trophy Son

Disturbance House calls, known as Domestics in the movies, are a real PITA. You never know what's going to happen. Domestic disturbance calls injure many officers and far too often kill one.

When you work a wagon, however, they are part of your general fare because these calls require two officers, and wagons are the only vehicles always two-man.

Most of the time, we could talk our way through these and calm everyone down so we could retreat. Sometimes, it involved negotiations, and sometimes, the only way to stop it was to remove one of the principals.

As I indicated in Chapter 38 – *Go to Radio* – many of them started with, "Get this motha-fucka out my house."

The mf was usually a drunk, usually a male, and we would either sweet-talk him out or, if all else failed, strong-arm him out and give him a place for the night.

We could usually get him out the easy way.

Some calls were in full swing when we arrived. A *battle royale* already in progress. This was one of those. We could hear the screaming from the street. The front door was open, which was common when someone called the police. They would open it, just in case.

We stepped into a scene with a young man screaming and threatening his mom and family. He saw us and redirected the invective to us, never a good sign.

I called to his mom, "Is he drunk?"

She said, "No, he's crazy, and he won't take his medicine."

We watched him for a second. He ran around the living room couch and began to climb on the furniture. He went behind the couch, jumped over the back and after bouncing off the cushions, went to a chair and did a little dance.

Barry and I looked at each other, we knew what to do. If we let him go on like this, he was going to hurt someone or himself and was going to destroy the house.

We nodded a signal and went toward him.

He saw us coming, jumped over the couch again, and ran through the dining room, grabbing a trophy off a bookcase as he went.

The trophy was one of those 1970s sports trophies with wooden pillars separating six-inch marble slabs, held together by foot-long threaded steel rods. There was a metal figure on top. Overall, a formidable hand-held weapon in the hands of a crazy person.

We chased him into the kitchen. He ran around the table to the far side. Barry and I came from opposite directions to split his attention and attack him from his blind side if he decided to attack one of us.

He chose me. He raised the trophy over his head and faced me as I came around the table. I raised my stick, but before I could do anything, the trophy exploded.

Barry reached him with his signature speed, hit the trophy, obliterated it, and scared him so bad he burst into tears!

He said he wasn't scared but upset about the broken trophy, but believe me, he was shit scared.

We handcuffed him, got his meds from Mom and took him to the catchment center. We dropped him off, gave the meds to the nurse and resumed patrol.

Barry was driving and could sense my eyes on him. We were silent since leaving the house. Sometimes, it takes a while to unwind from these battles.

He looked over and said, "What?"

I said, "That was amazing. I never saw anything like it. You were incredibly fast, and the accuracy in hitting the trophy, well... I could never have done that."

He paused, looked at me sideways and said, "I was aiming at his *head*."

We laughed.

I said, "Come on."

He said, "Really, I was aiming at his head. The trophy just got in the way."

We laughed again and debriefed about the outcome. There were no good guys, and no bad guys hurt – the optimum result.

And, our man was where he belonged, where he could get his meds and chill out.

Chapter 87

Give Me that &$.#*. Car

"Of mines I little know, myself,

But just the names of gems, -

The colors of the commonest,

And scarce of diadems"

- Emily Dickinson

On the way to work one afternoon in what was supposed to be a free-fly-zone. I stopped at a red light, and there was a man on the corner, chillin or hanging out or holding up the utility pole. I wasn't sure which. He called out to me, "Hey, gimme that motha fuckin' car."

He was working with a partner. Apparently, this type of duty required two.

It was nice weather; my window was down.

I wasn't quite sure I was hearing correctly so I responded for clarification with equal erudition.

I shouted back a throaty, obnoxiously nasal, dragged-out, "Huuuuuhhh?"

He said, "Gimme that motha fuckin' car."

I said, "Come and get it."

I had not yet read *The Hot Gates*[39]. I came up with that snappy retort all on my own.

When he started to walk toward the car, I reached for my pistol. His friend grabbed his arm. He leaned over to his ear and whispered something.

His bud bugged and returned to the sidewalk.

I waited for a few seconds and said, "Well?"

He said something else clever but stayed on the sidewalk.

I drove off.

In the locker room, I was telling the story when one of the other officers, who always made a caustic comment, said, "Yeah, Cubbage. I'm sure people are standing in line to steal that Nova."

I guess this insults normal people. I think that's what this was meant to do. Asperger's don't work that way. I wondered what it even meant.

As Emily's poem illuminates, shiny objects are not interesting to us. Well, me anyway.

But this lad apparently put great stock on what car someone drives. He didn't seem to worry much about where he lived, but the make and model of someone's car was a priority item. He drove a car way above my budget, and since he was married with kids, more so out of his.

I started to inquire what he thought the person's motivation was, if not the car, but thought better of it and went back to the business of getting ready for whatever drama awaited at the top of the locker room stairs and beyond.

When we got in the wagon, I asked Barry, "What's the deal with the comment about the car?"

[39] *The Hot Gates* by William Golding - 1965

He said, "You have to understand in his world the car is his expression of his worth to the world."

I said, "Then why does he live in a house worth less than his car?"

He said, "Because you can sleep in your car, but you can't drive your house. Also, the car is his only private space. It's a place where his wife can't go. Unlike you, he's the only one with a key to that car. He keeps money and other things hidden in it from his wife."

It was all too much. It was enough for me to try to keep all my group's social nonsense straight. Trying to process this for a different culture would have to wait.

Chapter 88

"That's Him"

I knew Donnie from the old neighborhood. He was a few years older, from what I call in my first book the minor-boom, which was enough for me to avoid him, but he was also constantly *wound-up* and a bit caustic, another reason to keep some distance.

Fast forward to the first year on the street. I knew Donnie was on the force but hadn't seen him in years. I was working with Barry when a call came out about a robbery. The description was:

Strong-arm robbery on the highway, committed by two males, #1, 6'2", wearing a green army jacket, blue jeans and white sneakers. #2, 5'2", wearing a white tee-shirt, blue jeans and sneakers.

We called this a *Mutt and Jeff* team. Mutt and Jeff was a comic in the newspaper at the time with characters called Mutt and Jeff, one was tall, and the other short.

A *strong-arm robbery* is a robbery of physical intimidation. The robbers physically frightened or beat up the person by hand to get them to relinquish their property.

You need to know, there was a uniform of the day. Whenever the uniform changed for the police, there were four of them, the dispatcher would let you know what the uniform of the day was for the day.

For the first few days after the change, the dispatcher would announce, "The *uniform of the day* is uniform number two, long sleeves, and tie," or whatever.

I began to think, *The bad guys also have a uniform of the day.*" I could never validate it, but I was convinced they coordinated what they wore to confuse the police. This event reinforced the thought.

After the robbery call, we scrambled around to find these two. Several cars came on the air to ask the dispatcher where to bring suspects. If you caught someone shortly after a robbery and near the scene of the robbery, you could have the complainant look at them.

If you caught the right person, they would say, "*That's him.*" and you would lock him up.

Barry and I were three blocks from the scene when we saw what we were sure were the robbers. We jumped out, nabbed them and drove them to the scene.

What we saw when we got there was ridiculous.

On the scene were a dozen or so police vehicles, our guys, a supervisor and a line team from Highway Patrol. Also, on the scene were seven, yes seven, identically dressed and matching Mutt and Jeff teams. I mean seven sets of two males, #1, 6'2", wearing a green army jacket, blue jeans and white sneakers. #2, 5'2", wearing a white tee-shirt, blue jeans and sneakers.

I looked around and thought, "What in the world?"

Barry looked at me with the same puzzled look.

We both said, "Uniform of the day."

That's when I heard a high-pitched voice say, "That's him."

It was Donnie. He was in a Highway Patrol uniform, standing next to his partner, laughing hysterically.

He was laughing and pointing to Mutt and Jeff teams one at a time, shouting, "That's him." "That's him." "That's him."

He was pleased with himself and found the whole thing amusing.

He was mocking *us* - the rookies, I immediately got my ass on my shoulders. Then I realized Donnie was short!

Standing there in his Highway uniform with the boots, britches, and crushed hat emphasized how short he was. Add the fact his partner was tall made it even more ironic.

Here, he was mocking us, with the Mutt and Jeff teams, as part of a Mutt and Jeff team himself.

Injustice began to creep in. Aspies as a group have a *real* problem with injustice, so much so it surfaces on standardized psychology testing.

To make it worse, although we caught every Mutt and Jeff team in the 17th wearing the uniform of the day, no one apparently caught the *right* one because the complainant failed to identify *any* of them.

This was a big letdown for us, and Donnie was making it worse.

Barry and I asked our team if they wanted a ride back to where we got them, and they said, "Yes."

We took them back and let them out.

About 45 minutes later, the dispatcher broadcast an assist call in the same area where we saw Donnie. We hit the lights and siren and rushed to the scene. When we arrived, there was a typical 17th District melee in the middle of the street.

Officers struggled with people, as a crowd formed with shouting and other chaos.

A couple of officers arrested one of the participants. They were putting the cuffs on him when a woman came into the crowd and started to shout. Apparently, the guy they were locking up was a relative.

Barry and I were at the edge of the crowd when the crowd surged and moved like a wave in our direction. I noticed Donnie and his partner moving toward the center. The woman grabbed one of the officers by the arm.

Quick as Pan, Donnie slapped her across the forehead with a sap. It was one of the flat ones. She went down like a sack of potatoes.

When she went down, rookies grabbed her and slapped handcuffs on her. They stood her up with her brand-new tattoo and turned and said, "Who hit her?"

Crickets.

I watched Donnie. He backed to the edge of the crowd, put the sap away and was snickering. The officer kept asking. Donnie kept sniggering, "That's him."

He was having fun with himself again. He was going to bag us with the hag he sapped and make fun of us while he did it.

Enough! We were all new. Donnie assumed no one knew who he was. In the confusion, no one knew which one of the uniforms hit the woman.

He was ramping it up now. Alternately pointing at the rookies and saying, "That's him." in his squeaky voice and laughing.

I started to walk toward him. Barry grabbed my arm. I looked at him and shook my head.

I said, "I'm OK, it's alright."

He let me go. We did this for each other. Kept each other out of trouble. He nodded and his expression showed he was with me.

I stepped up beside Donnie, close enough to touch him.

I said so only he could hear, "Gee Donnie, I wonder who it was who hit that old lady."

He froze. He looked like a turtle pulling his head inside its shell. I'm sure he would have if he could. He turned and looked at me. The look on his face said, "I know this guy, but I don't know from where."

He looked at my nameplate and cringed. He was trying now to remember if he was ever nasty to me so he could figure out what was going to happen next.

I looked at him and said, "What do you think? Do *you* know who hit her?"

His partner stepped to his side, and Barry stepped to mine. His partner got the familiar *holy-shit* look when he saw Barry.

I kept pressing Donnie. "My sergeant is over there now trying to figure out what happened."

I motioned toward my sergeant and said, "Have you met my sergeant? Have you heard about him?"

Everyone by now knew he was the one who threw the special units out of the 17th. Donnie and his partner put it together, I was the one who precipitated it.

Donnie's partner now put another few inches of distance between us. I laughed inside and thought, *"Don't ever play poker."*

Donnie just stood with his mouth open.

I said, "Come on, I'll introduce you to the sergeant."

"No, that's OK." he stammered.

He looked for his partner and realized he was on his own.

He looked back at me and said, "We better resume. I think this is under control."

I said, "Yes, that's probably a good idea. Why don't you do that? Listen, say 'Hi' to Jimmy for me if you see him."

Both bugged.

Donnie said, "Yeah, we will."

And quickly left.

Donnie probably changed for about 10 minutes or so, or at least enough time to get back to his car and leave the 17th.

I saw him a couple of times after that, but never in the 17th District.

Wonder why.

Chapter 89

"Watch Your Head"

"Drink your orange juice."

— *Plato's Mom*

Everybody has their pet peeves, their limits, their point of no return. Barry never reached the latter, but he did have one pet peeve, dead bodies. It made me wonder why he chose to work on the wagon because the dispatcher sent us to these twice a month, if not more. The dispatcher broadcast this one as *a hospital case*. We were back on day work. It was the first call of the day.

He said, "Well, they're waking up and realizing their sick. Let's go."

When we arrived, an elderly woman greeted us and said, "Old Joe didn't drink his orange juice this morning. He always drinks his orange juice. Would you see if he's alright?"

Old Joe was on the third floor, up we went. It was a good thing we were young.

Joe was in a darkened room, sitting in an overstuffed chair. The chair was facing away from the door, so when we walked in, Barry walked around to face him.

He started calling, "Sir, wake up."

The lady stayed in the doorway; I walked to the side of the chair.

Barry continued to try to wake Joe. We always carried gloves. When Joe didn't respond, Barry took his gloves and began to slap him to wake him up; the calls weren't doing it.

I already knew Joe was dead by the way his body sat. I put my hand on his. He was as cold as a popsicle. I tried to get eye contact with Barry, because my back was to the door where the lady stood. He was slapping Joe.

I said, "Barry."

He hit him again.

"Barry," I repeated.

"What?"

He knew as soon as he looked at me what I was trying to tell him.

He pulled back and said, "Oh, no."

I nodded and whispered, "Yeah, he's *been* dead, probably all night."

He looked at the floor and shook his head.

"First call." he moaned.

We always brought the stretcher just in case. I laid it on the floor.

Barry was still facing the door as we moved Joe to the stretcher. We were situating him on the stretcher, and I figured since he sat in this position for hours, his head, which was on his chest, was stuck there.

But when Barry laid his shoulders back, it released and hit the hardwood floor with a *bang!*

And the lady at the door softly said, "Watch his head."

We lost it. I was facing away from her, so I didn't have to hide it. Barry was struggling not to laugh and was giving me the stink eye because I was silently laughing in his face.

Then the lady softly said, "Do you think he's dead?"

I stood, composed myself and turned toward her. I was delicate because I still wasn't sure what the relationship was.

I said, "Yes, ma'am, I'm sorry, but he's passed."

There was a short silence, and she said, "I thought he might be dead. When he didn't drink his orange juice, I figured he probably was dead."

I kept my poker face and nodded. I told her we would take him to the Medical Examiner's office, where she could call to make arrangements.

She said, "Oh, he just lives here."

That meant he was a boarder, and she didn't care much at this point what happened. We took her info, got his info and took Joe to the ME.

I guess the moral of the story is: *Drink Your Orange Juice.*

Barry complained the whole way to the ME he was getting sick of dead people. Especially the first thing in the morning.

I sensed he might soon decide to end the partnership and move to a car. But he didn't have to. Someone called in a chit with the lieutenant, who was his neighbor; he wanted to work on a wagon.

The next week the lieutenant ordered the sergeant to assign him to the wagon with Barry, and me to a patrol car.

Barry told me he held on for as long as he could, but between the dead bodies and this new partner, he was getting off the wagon, too. He lasted another week and took an assignment on a solo car.

We missed the partnership, but neither of us missed the wagon. Shortly thereafter, Barry went to Stakeout, and I worked patrol car 1711 until I pissed the captain off enough that he sent me to work in a different squad.

That's a whole nother set of stories.

Chapter 90

"Take a Week Off"

"Hubris is back in town."

— W. C. Fields

At some point, we passed the one-year mark. The date passed without much notice by me, but the lieutenant was keeping book. Shortly after *his* calendar hit the one-year mark, he called me into the office. Wondering how I rated this honor, I greeted him and sat down.

He said, "Kid, have you taken a vacation yet?

I said, "No, sir."

"What are you waiting for? You have all the maximum accruable time in your bank. You need some time off."

"No, sir, I don't want to miss anything."

He laughed and said, "They'll be plenty of crime left by the time you get back. Get out of here and I don't want to see you until you've taken a full six days off. Give your schedule to the corporal."

I answered with a sad faced, "OK."

He laughed and said, "Kid, no one should work an entire year without a vacation. Go have some fun."

When I got home my wife could tell something was wrong.

Sorry, that probably gave you whiplash. Allow me to explain.

Remember the nurse with the shiny hair? It turns out her name is *Pat.*

Shortly after Field Training I got a call from an old girlfriend who, with good reason, began with, "Don't hang up!"

Then she said, "I have tickets for the ballet."

"I'm not taking you to the ballet."

"No, not me, my friend. I think you'll like her."

It took some convincing on her part, but I agreed to meet them at a club.

Fed up with the whole dating scene, I figured whatever it was that was different about me was having a negative effect, but I wasn't going to waste any more time figuring it out; it was too much trouble. I was still in the dark about Aspergers.

I was on a hiatus from dating, concentrating on police work. I also spent more time helping my dad in the family garage door business. When I showed up for this blind date, I didn't even bother to change. I washed my hands but didn't bother to change the dusty flannel shirt or work boots.

Guess who it was when I got to the club? I could tell she didn't remember me, but I sure as hell recognized her!

I tried to talk to her in this loud, smoky club, but something was troubling her. She got into an argument with the other girl and they decided to go to the ladies' room.

With little tolerance left for dating and less for drama, it was the ladies' room for them and the Irish Exit for me.

I chalked it up, but the past girlfriend wasn't having it. She called me again and said her friend wanted to talk. She gave me her number, and I called.

We – she rather – talked for two hours.

I listened.

I liked what I heard.

Our first date was in a popular restaurant in Center City. She liked to talk. Since I like to listen, it was a good match. I also liked to look at her, and listening comes with a license to look.

She had the most beautiful face ever! I did get the sense something was missing. I couldn't quite put my finger on it at first, but then it hit me.

On that well-scrubbed cherubic face, with its flawless skin, cobalt blue eyes, apple cheeks and butterfly eyelashes, *there was no makeup.* No foundation, no rouge, mascara or grease paint.

She wasn't even wearing lipstick.

I hadn't seen a female with no makeup on her face since grade school.

Striking doesn't begin to describe her.

Apparently, everyone else thought so too because I couldn't help but notice as we walked to our seats every head in the place turned to look. Some couldn't help but stare.

While we were eating, and she was in mid-bite *and* mid-sentence, she whipped her head to the right and belted, *"What* the *fuck* are you looking at?!"

Followed by the sound of a fork hitting the floor.

I turned to see the guy reaching to pick up the fork she scared right out of his hand. I could also see his wife peering around the side of her booth.

I said, "What was that all about?"

Pat said, "He's been *staring* at me since we sat down."

Her voice carries, by the way.

Pat went right back to her dinner, never missing a bite, and as if it all were happening as one choreographed moment: while the starer's wife was shouting, "Oh, so you've been staring at *her*, have you?!" a waiter with a dessert trolly walked by the table, and Pat hollered, "Stop him!"

As the wife browbeat her husband and I sat in amazement, Pat perused the dessert tray, made her selection and, smiling, said, "What will you have?"

With all this happening at once, and notwithstanding my disappointment that she, all 4'9", eighty pounds of her, was finishing everything on her plate, the voices inside my head sang a chorus of, *"We like this girl."*

I had one wish: to change her last name.

A short time later – a quick visit to City Hall – I got my wish!

When I came home the day the lieutenant sent me on vacation, she said, "What's wrong?"

She could see something was bothering me.

I told her and she ran from the living room. I followed her into the bedroom, where she was pulling clothes from the dresser and putting them on the bed next to a suitcase. I don't know where she got the suitcase or how she got it out so fast.

She was now multi-tasking, filling the suitcase saying, "Where are we going?"

She was funny. I could have said anything, and she would have responded, "OK."

She really likes to travel.

We settled on Wildwood because it was close. We knew the owners of one of the hotels there. I knew we could get a room on short notice.

So, we gathered up our stuff and spent the next week in sunny Wildwood, N.J., eating boardwalk fries, ice-cream waffles, cotton candy and other delicacies.

I could get her into *Urie's*, Wildwood's famous seafood restaurant, once or twice as long as she didn't have to eat any fish.

Then it was amusement mayhem, miniature-golf (where I would hide when she hit the ball), tireless shopping on the boardwalk and Pacific Avenue (why they would name a street three blocks from the Atlantic Ocean, Pacific Avenue is anyone's guess, probably the same people who picked *The Burrs* as my high school mascot) and all Greek diners along the way because they served the best rice pudding.

The first time we visited Wildwood together (Pat was never there; she's from, *wait-for-it* - Brooklyn), she said, "I love amusements. The worse they are, the better I like them."

Remember the AS stereotype about taking things literally? I wanted my wife to be happy, so I first took her on this thing called the *Maelstrom* or something equally disgusting. She got on with a smile, and as it turned upside down, she screamed, "I *hate* you for bringing me on this ride."

I almost wet myself laughing. A disaster when you're upside-down.

I said, "Let me make it up to you. There's another one that's fun but not anywhere near as scary."

While apologizing, I walked her into the building, I distracted her from the name at the entrance. It was inside a large wooden building, so people couldn't see what was happening. I kept up the ruse until we were inside and past the name.

This one's name was *Hell Hole*. It was like a giant clothes dryer facing up.

She said, "What does this do?"

I said, "Oh, it's nice. It just spins around a little. It will give you a chance to relax after the last one."

She unwound and said, "OK."

We stood against the inner wall as the ride got underway, and as it began to spin, she said, "Oh, this is nothing."

Hubris was back in town.

It spun up momentum, I watched her face. She was looking around, as it slowly accelerated with that unsatisfied look one gets when something is boring. It continued to accelerate, and as she felt the Gs beginning to hold her to the wall, she said, "Is this all it does?"

Suddenly, her eyes widened, she looked at her feet, and the floor dropped out!

Her first instinct was to grab me to keep from falling, but we were all stuck to the walls because it was spinning so fast. She realized she wasn't going to fall and started screaming.

First a yell, then that lovely fluid invective that endears us to all New Yorkers.

I lost count of all the curse words and insults by the time she passed a dozen. My face ached from laughing. Between the Hell Hole sucking me against the wall and her constant swearing, my jaw hurt like a visit to the dentist.

When the floor finally returned and the ride wound to a stop, she ran to the exit and out onto the boardwalk.

"Let's go," she shouted. "I don't like these rides."

I said, "But you said the worse, the better."

If looks could kill….

Two cobalt daggers told me I'd better shut up.

I calmed her down and said, "OK, let's get a cheese steak."

That got her attention. She looked at me and stopped.

"OK," she said, "But no more stupid rides."

"OK," I agreed as we walked off to the restaurant.

It's hard for anyone to resist a cheese steak. Pat couldn't. Apparently, they don't have good ones in Brooklyn.

That was 48 years ago and counting.

Chapter 91

What?!

"Occasionally he stumbled over the truth, but hastily picked himself up and hurried on as if nothing had happened."

— *Sir Winston Churchill*

I can't imagine what it's like to be the captain of a police district. A district full of rookies must be particularly challenging, and everyone has their thresholds. Ours was reaching his.

After all my time on this side of the lens, my advice to any Aspie thinking of taking a job managing normal people would be: ***"Don't even think about it."***

After a refreshing week at the seashore, my favorite thing, I was back to my second most favorite thing, the 17th District. That's not sarcasm, and I am capable despite the stereotype to the contrary. I enjoyed uniform police work. I was anxious to get back.

But, when I walked back into the district on the first day of daywork, the sergeant said, "The captain wants to see you after roll call."

I'm told by normal people that should have rattled me.

My reaction was a flat, "OK."

After roll call, I walked to the captain's office and entered the outer office. The captain was on the phone in his office to the left. In front of me was the captain's clerk's desk. The clerk was affectionately known as his flunky. I didn't make that up, it came from someone else.

Anyway, when I walked in the clerk was talking to another officer, and they both looked at me with the *someone's-dog-died* look. The best I could get from the *look* was, "Something's wrong."

The other officer was the head of the clique from *The Magic Memo* chapter, who had been whispering in the captain's ear about me.

With a stern look, the clerk said, "Wait here."

He went into the captain's office; the captain hung up his phone and *ran* to the outer office.

He looked at me with disgust and said to his man, "Where is that *list of questions* I gave you?"

He frantically looked around the clerk's desk until he found the list.

The list was a quarter page of looseleaf paper with torn edges. On it was *one* word printed in large red block letters.

"WHAT."

He grabbed it up in a theatrical flourish, like he had discovered the Rosetta Stone, whipped around, looked up at me and shouted, "WHAT?!"

I looked alternately at him and the two Cheshire Cat bobbleheads. I refocused on the captain, searching for some clue as to *what* was going on.

He didn't even bother to tell the uninvolved officer to leave. A clear violation of *Management 101*.

I said, "*What*, what?"

I didn't have much to go on and being literal, with no other point of reference, it was all I could come up with.

He slammed the *list* down on the desk and said, "*What* were you thinking?"

He began pacing around the office, throwing his hands in the air saying, "You're going to the front[40] for this. I'll be surprised if you're not arrested."

I said, "I'm still not following."

The captain said, "Give me the folder."

The clerk gave him a folder and me a gloomy look, slowly shaking his head, highlighting my hopeless predicament.

The captain said, "Your photo was picked out of a photo display."

I said, "What are you talking about?"

He said, "Last week, you were involved in an incident where people went to the hospital after you assaulted them."

I said, "You showed people my picture?"

He got more angry and red-faced because, as an Aspie, I had focused on the wrong thing.

He screamed, "Who are you talking to?! Yes, we showed your picture." showing me the picture in the file. It was my academy photo.

I said, "You showed my academy photo in a lineup?"

He shouted, "Yes, that's not the point. The point is you hit a woman who is now in the hospital, and the people there picked you out of the photo display."

I said, "When did this happen?"

He said, "Wednesday."

"Last week?"

"Yes, what about it?"

---

[40] The Front was cop talk for the department's internal Trial Board. If you violated some departmental rule or procedure a supervisor could *take you to the front*.

I said, "I was off last week. I wasn't even in the city last week."

They froze. My confused look must have been contagious because we were all wearing it now.

The captain said, "What?"

I was in synch with this particular *what* and said, "I was out of the city all last week. The lieutenant sent me on vacation. Did anyone bother to check the attendance sheet before accusing me of all this?"

Stymied, afraid to remonstrate me for the snarky remark, they looked at one other.

The captain, God love him, said, "Are you sure?"

I reached into my pocket and produced my *regulation-bound notebook*.

I asked, "What was the date?"

He provided the date.

I flipped through the notebook and said, "Yes from date *x* to date *y*, vacation. It's on the daily attendance report and the time-bank reconciliation as a withdrawal of six days' vacation time."

"And, by all means, ask the lieutenant."

Realizing how disorganized they were, I was leading them. And I didn't care how flippant it sounded because they were tampering with my career and freedom.

The captain stood bug eyed for a moment, and I could tell the thought occurred to him to challenge my remarks about the attendance report, but he recovered.

He turned to the clerk and said, "See what I've been saying about the importance of these notebooks."

He turned to me, slapped me on the arm and said, "Good work. You can go."

No, *sorry*, or *we made a mistake* or explanation of what he intended to do about the *investigation* that tagged me as a felon while I vacationed in the next state over.

Not to mention disciplining me in front of one of my peers.

Nothing.

I looked around at them, hesitating on each face. I left, but not before a recurring theme sounded inside my head:

"What the hell have I done to myself now?!"

The End of Volume One

Opening to Volume II

Thrusting yourself into police work can be challenging. Being thrust into police work with other freshly minted rookies directly from the academy, with no veteran police officers to break you in, is a severe challenge.

Doing this with undiagnosed Asperger syndrome – challenging to the nth degree.

I recently saw an ad for safety equipment in which a retired police officer professes in two and a half decades of police work, he never once intervened in a rape, home invasion, or robbery.

I don't know where *he* worked, but I checked all those boxes in the first few months.

In addition to *all the above,* I experienced shootings, stabbings, burglars, blizzards and horse chases.

And it wasn't about to slow down any time soon. This volume starts as I return from my first vacation, forced by my lieutenant, because I didn't want to miss anything.

He was right when he told me, "They'll be plenty of crime left by the time you get back."

When I came back and jumped on the still-spinning *merry-go-round* of police drama, it was clear the lieutenant should have added:

"You ain't seen nothing yet!"

www.ingramcontent.com/pod-product-compliance
Lightning Source LLC
Chambersburg PA
CBHW060408130626
46555CB00005B/2008